THE FAMILY NEXT DOOR

CAROLINE FINNERTY

Boldwood

First published in Great Britain in 2023 by Boldwood Books Ltd.

Copyright © Caroline Finnerty, 2023

Cover Design by Head Design Ltd

Cover photography: Shutterstock

A CIP catalogue record for this book is available from the British Library.

Paperback ISBN 978-1-80162-555-5

Large Print ISBN 978-1-80162-556-2

Hardback ISBN 978-1-80162-554-8

Ebook ISBN 978-1-80162-557-9

Kindle ISBN 978-1-80162-558-6

Audio CD ISBN 978-1-80162-549-4

MP3 CD ISBN 978-1-80162-550-0

Digital audio download ISBN 978-1-80162-553-1

Boldwood Books Ltd
23 Bowerdean Street
London SW6 3TN
www.boldwoodbooks.com

For Tom, my sunshine.

1

_____

I watched yer man emerge from the house next door at exactly twenty-two minutes past eight. He was running late this morning. He stopped to inspect the paintwork on his black Audi, buffing it with his thumb. He was dressed in skintight tracksuit bottoms that left little to the imagination and even though it was November, and there was frost twinkling on the ground, he wore a T-shirt. He always wore a T-shirt; I don't think the man even owned a coat. He liked showing off his bulging biceps; I don't know why because he had them destroyed with tattoos. Mr Muscle is what I call him.

He got into his car and reversed out of the driveway. Then herself came out a few minutes later, all big blonde hair and make-up, dressed up to the nines in stiletto heels and practically pushing the child down the driveway in her hurry to get into her car. They were always rushing everywhere those two. Always late. She opened the back door for the little girl to climb in, then she sat in the front seat, started the engine and she was gone too. I wouldn't see them until after five o'clock that evening.

I still didn't know their names even though I had been living there for almost nine months by then. We had moved in around the same time, but they had immediately set about renovating the house, replacing the old with the new. Their house was like all the other houses on the street with their modern windows and colourful front doors. Now my house was the only one left with the original timber windows. They had taken up the crumbling tarmac in the driveway and replaced it with biscuit-coloured resin and when I looked out the back bedroom window, my view was obstructed by a glass box extension where they had broken through the wall of their kitchen. They had dug up all the grass in the garden and replaced it with artificial stuff, then of all the things they could have done, didn't they go and build a bar in the garden. A bar! They had spent the tail end of the summer hosting their friends, sitting out late into the night laughing and drinking and keeping me awake with their antics.

I waited until the car had disappeared down the road, then I moved away from the window, letting the net curtain swing back into place. I took Dora's lead off the banister in the hall and clipped it on to her collar and we headed for our morning walk.

Dora had arrived on my doorstep last February just a few days after I had moved in. I woke one morning and heard scratching at the front door. It had put the heart crossways on me. I had hurried down the stairs, opened it and there she was sitting on the step looking up at me with a note of impatience as if she was saying, *Where the hell have you been? I've been waiting for you all this time to let me in.* She looked at me with the saddest brown eyes I've ever seen. Even though she was a dog, I felt as though she could see inside my soul. I bent down to have a closer look at her and saw she was in a right sorry state. I don't know what breed she is; the vet reckons she's some kind of cross between a Yorkshire terrier and a Jack Russell. Her wiry hair was matted, and her claws were long and growing around into the pads of her paws. She had no collar on her, and she was grey around the muzzle, so I knew she wasn't a puppy.

'Well, look at you!' I whistled, shaking my head. Then, just as I was feeling sorry for her, didn't the cheeky fecker go around my ankles and walk straight into the house like she owned the place!

'Oh, no you don't; go on, get out of here,' I told her, but Dora took no notice of me. I decided to take her to the vet to see if they had any reports about a missing dog. They scanned her and told me that she wasn't microchipped. The vet explained that she would have to be surrendered to a rescue centre, but God damn it, when I looked into her sad little eyes, I couldn't do it to the poor girl, so she came home with me.

'It's only temporary,' I warned her. 'Don't be getting yourself comfy. It's just till we can find you a proper home.'

I called her Dora, after *Dora the Explorer*. When Tim – he's my key worker – called for a visit later that week he was taken aback to see Dora snoozing on the sofa.

'You got a dog?' he asked in bewilderment.

I told him what had happened and how it was only until I found her a home. Tim said that maybe I should hold on to her, that she'd be good company for me. I told him that I was nervous of having something being reliant on me; I was worried it would be too much pressure. Tim told me to give it a week or two and see how it went and Dora has stayed by my side ever since. There's no minding in her in fairness. She eats, she does her business, I bring her for a little walk, and she waits outside tied to the lamp post while I go into the shop, then she spends the rest of her time curled up asleep on her chair. It's a dog's life, I tell you.

By the time Dora and I get home from our walk, it's time to clean up the place and do my laundry, then sure it's lunchtime. After lunch I usually make myself a cup of tea and stick on the TV. On this day, I was just settling in to watch *Judge Judy* with a cuppa when the doorbell rang. Dora, who was snoring loudly in her spot on the sofa beside me, raised her head and pricked up her ears.

'Who is it now?' I asked, rolling my eyes. We were hardly inundated with visitors. She jumped up and followed me out to the door. I caught sight of myself in the hall mirror. I was starting to look and feel every one of my fifty-four years; the greys were taking over my natural auburn colouring and a starburst of lines spread out from the corners of my eyes. I turned away from the mirror and peered through the spyglass. I didn't recognise the official-looking young woman standing there. She was very glamorous, dressed in a skirt suit and high heels. Maybe she was one of my neighbours? I kept the chain on just in case, before I opened it.

'Hi Eileen, we haven't met. I'm Savannah, I work on the outreach team,' she said, introducing herself.

Was it that time already? I did a quick calculation and realised she was right. The days were flying by.

'What happened to Tim?' I asked, removing the chain. An icy draft rushed inside. I was used to dealing with him but this new girl had thrown me. Tim calls around every month to check up on me. He wants to see that I'm eating and taking my meds and not living in squalor, but I always keep the place clean and tidy. It's usually a ten-minute job: he ticks his boxes and off he goes again until the following month. He used to visit weekly when I first moved in, but he said I'm making good progress.

'He's off on leave I'm afraid,' Savannah explained, 'so I'm covering his clients while he is out.'

'More's the pity,' I said, looking Savannah up and down. She looked far too young to be a member of the workforce. I'd say she was just out of college. 'I suppose you want to come in?'

'Well, yes…' She nodded. 'I won't keep you too long.' She seemed nervous. Her eyes darted around and her hands were fidgeting with the strap on her handbag.

I led her into the living room, picked up the remote and silenced the TV. Then I gestured for her to take a seat. She quickly inspected the sofa before tucking her skirt beneath her and sitting down.

'Oh, not there,' I said quickly.

'Sorry?' she said, jumping up again, looking terrified.

'That's where Dora sits,' I told her.

'Oh…' She stood up and moved down to the other end. 'Is this okay?'

I nodded. Dora hopped up onto her spot beside her. Savannah looked warily at her.

'Don't worry, she won't bite. She's very friendly.'

Nonetheless, Savannah kept her elbows tucked in as she unclipped her briefcase and took out a notepad. She reminded me of a little bird.

'So how are you doing, Eileen?' she began.

'All good.'

She looked around the room. 'The place is looking well.'

'The rubbish isn't piling up if that's what you're worried about,' I quipped.

Savannah gave me an uneasy smile and started writing something on her clipboard.

'That was a joke,' I added. The last thing I wanted was Tim getting a report back that I had been unco-operative.

Savannah tucked her hair behind her ears. 'You're settling in well then?' she continued. 'Have you met any of the neighbours yet?'

'Not yet.'

'Well, it's only been a little while, still lots of time to make friends.' She smiled.

'It's been nine months.'

'Has it?' Savannah said absently, scribbling something else in her notes. 'Time flies. And everything else is okay?'

'It's all hunky-dory.'

'Okay... well, everything looks good to me,' she said, the relief in her voice to be finished with me clearly audible. She stood up and brushed Dora's hairs off her wool skirt. 'I'll leave you to get back to your show.' She nodded at the TV screen frozen on Judge Judy's courtroom. 'You have the number for the office if you need anything.'

By the time Savannah left, dusk was beginning to fall, and my tea had gone cold. The street was starting to get busy again and one by one the houses began lighting up as people started returning home from work. I saw the man from next door arrive home soon after with the little girl, and herself came home a little while later. Then the noise started up. The TV would be blaring, and the juicer would be whizzing, or they would start hoovering. Always making a racket they were.

Dora stood at the door and whined.

'Do you need to go out, love?' I asked.

I put her on the lead and then took her out to do her business in the front garden. The full moon looked watery in the foggy night air and frost-tipped grass crunched under my slippers. Dora was taking her time sniffing around.

'Come on, old girl,' I encouraged, shivering. 'It's too cold to be moseying about tonight.'

The light was on in the living room next door so I could see in through the darkness while I waited for Dora. Himself was standing at the cooker while the little girl was playing with a toy kitchen. She was pretending to pour tea from a miniature teapot. I often stood watching them from my garden. Sometimes they would be all curled up together on the sofa watching TV or helping one another to prepare dinner at their huge kitchen island. I don't know why I did it to myself because I always felt a stab in my heart at the cosiness of it all. The contentment of it. I ran my fingers along the links of my bracelet, the only thing I had left from my old life. I had once had all of that. I had had a family too and then I had gone and thrown it all away.

2

Lucy Walsh turned her Mini Cooper on to St Brigid's Road and drove along under the orange glow of the halogen street lamps until she reached her house, number 28. The sight of her home filled her heart with pride. Their front door, which she had recently painted marshmallow pink, made her smile every time she saw it. Her five-year-old daughter Anabel had chosen the colour and at first Lucy had been unsure, but now she adored its cheery frivolity. She still couldn't believe they lived on this road. Houses here were in demand and whenever a property came on the market, there would be a queue of people a mile long down the street just to view it.

She was still pinching herself that they were homeowners. Her parents had never owned their own home, they had always rented, and she and her brothers had lived in various properties all her life, moving on when the landlord wanted to sell the place or if the rent was increased. They had never been allowed to put their own stamp on things. Growing up, she had been warned not to stick posters up in her bedroom and her mother had been too nervous to hang pictures around the home in case they would mark the wall and they would lose their deposit at the end of the tenancy. As a result, nowhere that they had lived had ever really felt like home. So, she was proud of herself and Neil for being able to save enough to buy their own place.

Lucy was a freelance make-up artist and Neil worked as a personal trainer. He owned his own gym and, between the two of them and sheer hard work, they had been able to scrape enough money together to purchase this two-up, two-down house on St Brigid's Road. It had been in a sorry state when they had bought it; that was the only reason they were able to afford it. Before them, the ex-council house had been lived in by an old lady who had eventually moved into a nursing home. She had purchased it outright from Dublin Corporation in the 1980s and it seemed she had done nothing to it since then. The windows had been leaking, and the flowery wallpaper peeling from the mildew-spotted walls. They had opened a wardrobe to find it sprouting with mushrooms. But despite all of that, they had seen potential. Even when their families had told them they were mad to take on a house in such a poor state of repair, they could only see the family home that this house could be. With a bit of TLC and elbow grease, Lucy had known they could create their forever home.

As soon as they had been given the keys to number 28, they had set about renovating the house. They had knocked down the ground floor wall leading to the garden and added on a three-sided glass extension to allow light to flood into a large open-plan kitchen and living area. They had replaced the leaking windows with modern Aluclad frames in anthracite grey. The wallpaper had been stripped and the walls painted a soft white. They had pulled up the lino that covered the entire downstairs and replaced it with a polished concrete floor. She loved their house and the home they had created inside its walls.

Neil's Audi was already parked in the drive, so she parked behind him. She silenced the engine and sat for a moment, thinking about the conversation with him that she had planned for that evening. Recently,

Lucy had started to broach the subject of them having another baby. Annie was five now; the years were flying by. When Anabel was younger, they had been saving hard to buy their own house, so the timing had been wrong, but now they had their house, they had finished their renovation and still Neil didn't want to entertain the idea of them having another child. He kept saying that they had a nice life and with only two bedrooms, the house was too small; where would they put another baby? They could share, Lucy had suggested. She had shared a bedroom with her brother until she was thirteen. It wasn't ideal, especially if the siblings were a girl and a boy, but it would be fine when they were small, and they could figure something out by the time they got older. But then Neil had changed tack and argued that they couldn't afford for Lucy to take maternity leave; she was self-employed, her business was going well, if she took a break now her clients might find another make-up artist. Her head told her that Neil was right; the two of them being self-employed didn't give them any security. Her career was going from strength to strength at the moment, but her clients might forget all about her if she took maternity leave.

Then there was the money side of things; between the mortgage and the loan they had taken out for the renovations, there wasn't much left over at the end of every month. Financially, how *would* they manage on Neil's salary? The gym business was precarious; it seemed there were always new competitors springing up every week and it was getting harder to retain customers. She told Neil that she would take three months' maternity leave and go back to work early but, even as she'd said the words, she knew it wasn't realistic; there was no way she would have been ready to leave Anabel when she had been that young. He had countered that by asking how they would afford the crèche fees to mind the baby. He always had a perfectly sensible response for every argument she put forward. Although she knew he was right – financially, it made no sense for them to have another baby – her heart ruled her head and Lucy still longed to give Anabel a little brother or sister. On her way home she had stopped in SuperValu and bought a bottle of his favourite red wine to open once Anabel was in bed. She was hoping that the wine would put him in a good mood and relax him before she broached the topic once more.

She opened the door and stepped out of the car. As she fished her house keys from her handbag, her eyes landed on the tatty PVC door of number 26, where their reclusive neighbour resided. The house was in a sorry state and was the only one on the street that hadn't been modernised. Neil was always complaining that no matter how much work they did on their own home or how much money they spent doing their place up, having 'Mad Mary' next door – that was their nickname for her because they didn't know her real name – brought down the appearance of their house; in fact, it brought down the whole street. Her grass was so long that it was almost knee height and she still never bothered to cut it. After spending weeks moaning to Lucy about it during the summer, Neil had eventually called next door and offered to cut it for her himself because he couldn't stand it any longer but Mad Mary had given him short shrift and told him she could manage her garden 'perfectly fine'. Neil had come back into their house afterwards, fuming. He had called her a 'grumpy bitch'. Then a few weeks ago he had caught her dog using their drive to do its business and when he had called over to complain, Mad Mary had shut the door in his face. It incensed Neil that she clearly got her house for free from the council but then was too lazy to maintain it. He said that it wasn't fair that everyone else on their street worked so hard and put so much effort into keeping the street looking well and her unkempt house smack bang in the middle of the road undid all their hard work.

Lucy put her key in the lock, let herself in the front door and made her way down the hall and into the open-plan living area.

'Mammy!' Anabel cried, running to meet her as she entered the kitchen. Neil had collected her from the after-school childcare service they used. Lucy picked her up and swung her around their minimalist kitchen before placing her down again after a moment. She was getting heavy. She was growing fast; another sign that time was going too quickly, she thought.

'Hi, love,' Neil called over his shoulder as she entered the kitchen. 'How was your day?' He was standing at the quartz-topped island chopping vegetables. The winter evening lurked dark and shadowy beyond the glass bifold doors at the end of the room where a large L-shaped sofa was positioned opposite an inset stove.

'Good,' she said, ducking her head under the strap of her bag as she took it off and placed it in the cloakroom.

'Come have a cup of tea,' Anabel said, sliding her small hand into Lucy's own.

Lucy followed her over to where they had made a

little play area for her. Using some shelving from IKEA, she had cordoned off some space for Anabel in the corner of the kitchen. Neil hated mess and would get worked up if the house was untidy. Lucy always joked that Neil had a touch of OCD but since Anabel had arrived, he had got worse. He couldn't cope with her handprints on their navy high-gloss cupboards, or if her toys were left strewn around the place it would send him into a cleaning frenzy. They would be just about to sit down and watch something on Netflix when he would have to jump up and get a cloth to polish a smudge that Lucy hadn't even noticed. He would order Anabel to tidy up after herself, but Lucy was always telling him that she was a child and she was going to make a mess, that that was what kids did, it was how they learnt and explored the world, but he disagreed and said she was old enough to start tidying up after herself.

Lucy had two younger brothers and, growing up, her house had been full of noise and mess. There were always toys littering the floor or clothes strewn around the place in her house, whereas Neil had been an only child and he said his home had always been neat and orderly. He claimed he had never missed out by not having siblings but sometimes Lucy wondered if he would have been as neurotic about everything if he had grown up in a chaotic house like she had? Now Anabel automatically put away her toys when she was finished playing, without being asked. For a five-year-old, she was remarkably tidy, and Lucy hoped she wouldn't grow up to be a neat freak like her father.

Anabel handed her a tiny china teacup and Lucy pretended to sip from it. After a while, she left Anabel to play alone, then she took the cordless Dyson out and moved it around the floor. Neil liked to have the place clean before they sat down for dinner. A few minutes later, she noticed that he was waving to get her attention over the noise of the vacuum, so she turned off the Dyson.

'Did you sign for a parcel from Amazon yesterday?' he asked.

'No, I didn't see anything.'

'It says on the tracking information that it was delivered and signed for.'

'Maybe it was left next door while we were in work?' she suggested.

'Yeah, Mad Mary probably took it. Although God only knows what she'd want with a protein shaker.'

'Do you want me to go check with her?' Lucy offered.

He put his palms together gratefully. 'Would you

mind? If I go round there again, she'll probably set her dog on me.'

Lucy laughed. 'Sure. I'll just finish this, and I'll go over then.' She was happy to help. She needed to keep him in a good mood for the discussion she wanted to have later.

3

They were at it again. They'd get home from work and the hoover would start banging off the walls as they began cleaning. It was the same routine every day. I was trying to watch the six o'clock news but I could barely hear it over the racket coming from next door. Surely, their house didn't need to be vacuumed every day. I turned up the TV to drown out the noise. Eventually, it stopped and myself and Dora had just started to relax again, when I heard the doorbell go. I ignored it because no one ever called here at this time. It was probably the bloody Jehovah's Witnesses. When it rang again I looked over at Dora.

'I suppose I'd better answer it then,' I sighed. I got up from the sofa and headed out to the hall with Dora following after me. I checked through the spyglass and saw it was the woman from next door and the little girl was beside her. *This better not be about dog poo again...* It had happened once and the drama that Mr Muscle had made – you'd swear she'd shit in his cornflakes! Now, I always put Dora on her lead whenever she was doing her business. I picked Dora up and reluctantly opened the door.

'I'm Lucy from next door and this is my daughter Anabel,' the woman began. 'I don't think we've met properly.' She put forward her hand.

I took it limply in my own, not really sure what to do with it.

'I was just wondering if there was a parcel addressed to my husband left here, by any chance? It seems to have gone missing. It says it was signed for but I think these courier companies just fling them over the wall...' She gave a nervous laugh before lifting up a slim wrist and flicking her hair over to the side.

'No, there was nothing left here,' I said.

'Oh, okay thanks, I'll try number 30 then. It might have gone there.'

I reached up to close the door but the little girl stuck her hand out so that I almost caught her fingers.

'Can I rub your dog?' she asked, reaching out to

tickle Dora's ears. She was a pretty little thing with big blue eyes like her mother's and white-blonde wispy hair as fine as spun sugar.

'Careful, Anabel,' the mother warned. 'She could bite you!'

'I don't know if Dora is good with children,' I cautioned even though I knew she wouldn't hurt a fly but I was eager to have the pair of them gone from my doorstep. But of course, Dora betrayed me with her stubby tail eagerly pulsing from left to right. I placed her on the ground and the child bent down on her knees and started rubbing her ears. Then Dora turned over onto her back, belly up to the sky for Anabel to rub her. *Cheers Dora*, I thought.

'She's obsessed with dogs,' the mother explained, rolling her eyes. I noticed she had long purple nails with black hearts painted on them. Each nail was like an individual piece of art. Some people honestly have too much time on their hands...

Dora rolled back over and started licking the child's palm.

'It tickles, Mammy,' she giggled.

I have to say, she was a sweet little girl. I couldn't help but smile at her and Dora seemed to be enjoying the attention too.

Lucy and I stood awkwardly for a few moments while the little girl fussed over Dora.

'Right, well, we'd best head on and try and locate this package,' Lucy said after a minute. She reached for the little girl's hand. 'Come on, Anabel, let's go.'

'Bye, bye, Dora,' Anabel called over her shoulder as her mother led her down the drive back towards their own house.

I closed the door after them and felt my heart rate start to slow once more. *Lucy*, she had said her name was, and *Anabel* was the little girl. Tim would be proud of me for getting to know my neighbours. I'd have to tell him about it next time he called.

4

Lucy had eventually located the package in number 30. The house was owned by a friendly gay couple in their fifties called Theo and Chris who had invited them over with some of the other neighbours for drinks last Christmas. They had played charades and although Neil had little interest in party games, she and Anabel had loved it and Theo and Chris had been great hosts.

After dinner, she had given Anabel her bath and tucked her up in bed with a story. Then she had come back down the stairs, opened the bottle of wine that she'd bought earlier and poured them both a generous glass. They watched Netflix and she bided her time until Neil was on his second glass. She was hoping that the alcohol might have softened him somehow before she brought up the conversation that had been on her mind all day.

'Neil,' she began, holding her breath as she said the words. 'I've been doing some thinking...'

'Oh yeah?' he replied absently, not taking his eyes off the TV.

'I really think it's time we gave Anabel a brother or sister.' She finally spat it out.

The words seemed to hang in the air between them for ages before he finally exhaled heavily.

'What are you starting all of this again for, Lucy?' He sighed in exasperation.

'It's been on my mind for a while. Anabel is five now; I don't want her to be an only child and if we don't do it soon, the age gap between them will be too big,' she pleaded. Lucy was so close to her family. She saw her brothers all the time; they spent every Christmas together and were always at the end of the phone if she needed them. She wanted that same closeness for Anabel.

'I was an only child, and it didn't do me any harm,' he challenged.

She didn't dare say that, actually, she thought he could have benefitted from having a few siblings. He might not be so uptight about everything if he had. 'I know that,' she appeased instead, 'but she's always asking me if she can have a baby brother or sister.'

'Come on, Lu, we've been through it.' He tossed his hands up in the air. 'We've a great life as we are now. Why do you want another baby? Why would you want to change that?'

'I don't know… it just feels like something is missing,' she admitted. She couldn't explain it – on paper she had everything she had ever wanted. She knew she should be grateful to have Neil and Anabel, a lovely house and good job, but she still couldn't shake the longing to complete their family with another child.

'So, you're saying that Anabel isn't enough for you, is that it?' he retorted, twisting her words around into something ugly and not what she meant at all.

'Of course not. Anabel is my whole world, you know that! It's just that…' He had set her off balance, making her doubt herself, and she was struggling to explain it even to herself.

'Well, that's what it sounds like to me,' he cut across her, his voice climbing dangerously higher. 'Why can't you be happy with what you have? You're always looking for something more. Do you know how many people would kill for the life you have? Living here on one of the most sought-after streets in

Dublin, a lovely car parked outside and all the fancy stuff you could ever want?' he roared.

She stood up, keen to get away from him. She needed to defuse this fast. She was about to put her wine glass down on the island when she heard him coming behind her, then before she had time to prepare herself, she felt a force collide against her and she was falling. The glass smashed to the floor, the red wine splashing everywhere. She stumbled, her head banging against the quartz countertop before she fell to the ground. Pain blinded her. She could taste blood in her mouth. She tried to pick herself up, but she couldn't seem to coordinate her limbs. She tried again but she was too weak.

'Oh my God, are you okay? What have you done to yourself?' He hurried over beside her. Her head was spinning and when she looked at Neil there were two of him. Broken glass glistened angrily on the floor around them.

'I-I...' Her mouth was full of blood, and she couldn't get the words out. She spat onto the tiles and made a watery red pool on the floor beside the shards of glass and the spilled red wine. Her immediate thought was that she needed to clean it up before it stained. She tried to push herself up again with her arms, but they wouldn't support her.

'Mammy?' She heard Anabel's small voice enter the room. The noise must have woken her. 'Daddy, why are you shouting and why is Mammy on the floor?'

'Go back to bed, Anabel,' he warned, through gritted teeth.

'But I want to see what's wrong with my mammy.' Her voice quivered.

Lucy knew she needed to get up for Anabel's sake; she didn't want her daughter seeing her in this state, but she couldn't seem to coordinate her limbs to move. *Come on*, she told herself, *get up, get off the floor.* She flinched as Neil came towards her, put his hands beneath her shoulders and hoisted her into a seated position with her back resting against the island. The room spun and the floor shimmered around her. Her head was thumping, and she could taste a metallic tang in her mouth.

Anabel started to wail. 'She's bleeding, Daddy! Mammy's face is bleeding!'

'I'm okay, Annie,' Lucy managed to say but her tongue felt thick and swollen in her mouth and the words sounded strange to her.

'Your voice sounds funny.'

'She's fine, Anabel,' Neil replied in a deathly calm tone. How did he do it, she wondered. How was he able to be so calm and composed in this same moment she felt as though the bottom had been pulled out of her world?

Through her clouded vision she could see Anabel warily watching the scene from the sidelines. She had Dotty, the cloth comforter that she had slept with every night since she was a baby, wrapped around her hand as she sucked her thumb. She was a smart child; she knew something was wrong, but she didn't quite understand what or who was to blame.

'It's okay, Anabel,' Neil said in a kinder voice now. 'Mammy just slipped on the floor; it was wet and slippery.'

I saw the blurry outline of Anabel's face instantly relax.

'I'll go get Mammy a plaster for her sore face.'

'Good girl,' he encouraged.

Anabel returned moments later. 'I gotted you the plaster, Mammy,' she said as she knelt down on the floor in front of her and acted nurse.

'Thanks, love.' Lucy reached out and took it from her. Although she hadn't seen the wound herself, the blood that was trickling down along her chin told her that a Band-Aid wouldn't cut it.

'You'll be all better soon.' Anabel parroted the

same words that Lucy had so often said to her whenever she fell and hurt herself.

'Come on, Anabel, I'll take you back to bed,' Neil said after a bit.

While Neil was upstairs, Lucy put a hand up to her throbbing head and gingerly palpated her face. Her skin was tender to her touch and its contours didn't feel familiar; a mound now stuck out from above her eye socket, and her lip was swollen and sticky with what she knew was her own blood. Her whole body was trembling as the shock kicked in.

When Neil returned a few minutes later, he seemed composed. He reached for the tea towel hanging on the rail beside the sink. She winced as he tenderly dabbed at her face. She was shocked to see dark bloodstains seeping across the grey linen.

'God, look what you've done to yourself,' he muttered as he examined her, shaking his head. 'At least it doesn't seem to be too deep. Here, hold that up to your lip and I'll help you up.'

She did as he instructed and then he picked her up from the floor. He linked her arm and, as he led her over to the sofa, her legs felt wobbly and jelly-like as she walked.

'The floor must have been wet or something,' he

repeated as he began sweeping up the shards of broken glass.

She nodded, feeling numb. She was confused. It had all taken place so fast that she wasn't really sure what had actually happened; had he pushed her, or had she slipped?

'You know that I'd never do anything to hurt you,' he reiterated as if he could read her mind. He hugged her tightly, so tight that her wounded head stung as he pressed it against his shoulder, but she was afraid to ask him to let go.

* * *

Lucy's head was thumping when she woke the next morning. After they had cleaned up the mess in the kitchen, she and Neil had both gone to bed without any more discussion about what had happened. Neil had reached across the mattress and put his arm around her as he'd fallen asleep. He had snored softly beside her as she lay awake, tense and rigid, trying to remember the exact sequence of events that had left her lying on the floor. He said it had been an accident, but she wasn't so sure. Had his arm reached out to push her in the seconds before she fell or had she imagined it? He had washed the floor after dinner.

Sometimes he used too much detergent, so it could very well have been slippery. Eventually, she had fallen into a fitful slumber.

She got out of bed and went into their en suite. Neil had already left to open the gym and she was glad she didn't have to face him. She opened the bathroom cabinet and found some paracetamol. Punching out two tablets, she swallowed them without water. She caught sight of her face in the mirror. There was a small wound on her lip and a halo of bruising surrounded her eye. Although it was still quite puffy, she was relieved to see that most of the swelling had gone down overnight. She used her ring finger to lightly dab concealer over her bruised skin but even her skills as a make-up artist were unable to disguise the blue-black colour. She couldn't call in sick because she and her friend Jenna were booked in to do a bridal party and she would never let a bride down on the morning of her wedding, but her friend would be asking questions when she saw the state of her face. She knew she was going to have to come up with an excuse. As she ran a brush through her hair, the back of her head was still tender, and she could feel an egg-shaped lump underneath her hair.

After she was finished getting ready for work, she went into Anabel's room and woke her for school. She helped to put on her uniform, doing up the impossibly small buttons on her blouse and pulling her pinafore down over her head. If Anabel noticed her mother's bruised face, she didn't say anything about it. They went down to the kitchen together and as Anabel ate her Weetabix in painfully slow spoonfuls, she didn't mention what had happened the night before and Lucy didn't bring it up either. Lucy hoped that in her sleepy state she might have forgotten about it or perhaps she thought it had all been a dream.

5

When I looked out the window the next morning at the usual time, I saw Anabel being led down the driveway by her mother. The little girl looked adorable in her tartan school pinafore and bottle-green woollen jumper over a white blouse. Her hair was pulled up in two pigtails. As Lucy held her daughter by the hand, I thought back to when my own children were small, how my heart would swell plump in my chest as their hands reached up to mine. Those innocent eyes looking up at me, full of implicit trust that I would protect them from all the dangers in the world. But, as it had turned out, I was the one they had needed protection from...

Just then, Anabel spotted me through the net curtain, and she did something I wasn't expecting: she waved at me. As Lucy turned to open the door of her car for Anabel to climb in, I picked Dora up off the ground, pulled back the curtain so she could see us fully and used Dora's front paw to wave back at the child. She laughed and my heart exploded inside my ribcage. Her grin was good for the soul. She reminded me that there was still some goodness and purity left in the world, you just had to open your eyes to it.

As Lucy came around the car to climb into the driver's seat, I ducked to the side of the window, so she wouldn't see me watching them. I noticed that, despite the full face of make-up she had plastered on, she was sporting a shiner above her eye. That hadn't been there yesterday when they had called over. After Lucy and Anabel returned home, I had gone back inside and watched the news. Dora had curled up on the sofa beside me and begun snoring like a train as usual but, despite the decibels she was emitting, I had heard raised voices coming from next door. I had picked up the remote and lowered the volume on the TV to hear better. A voice had been shouting but the words were muffled through the walls, and I couldn't make out what was being said. Then I was sure I had heard someone crying. Was it Anabel? Or Lucy? I thought that maybe they were having an argument or perhaps Anabel had accidently broken something, and they were giving out to the poor child. Then something had crashed to the floor, followed by what sounded like a glass breaking. Dora had sat up on alert and pricked her ears. I looked at my little dog and she cocked her head back at me and gave a growl. She didn't like the sound of it either, but it hadn't seemed right to be eavesdropping like some kind of nosy neighbour. Whatever was going on was their business and nothing to do with me, so I had turned the volume up again and went back to watching the news, but now a niggling feeling of doubt filled me as I wondered if Mr Muscle had done this to her. I hoped I was wrong; maybe I was jumping to conclusions, but something told me that perhaps things weren't as perfect next door as they liked to portray from the outside...

6

As Lucy led Anabel up the path to school, she kept her head down and avoided making eye contact with the other parents. She returned to her car and then set off for Jenna's house. She and Jenna had arranged to travel to the bride's parents' house together. As she sat in the stalled M50 traffic, she began rehearsing in her head what she was going to say to her friend to explain the state of her face. She glanced at herself in the rear-view mirror. Although the bruising was definitely noticeable, with the help of her make-up skills, it was a lot better than it had been when she'd first looked in the mirror that morning. She hoped that maybe her friend might not notice anything.

'What on earth did you do to yourself, Lu?' Jenna

asked, cupping her hands over her mouth as soon as she got in the car.

It was not the reaction Lucy had been hoping for.

'I slipped. The floor was wet, and I banged into the island,' she said, exactly as she had rehearsed on the drive over. The lie – well, it wasn't really a lie; she still wasn't sure exactly what had happened – rolled off her tongue like butter curling off a knife.

Jenna sucked in sharply and leaned across the gearstick to take a closer look. 'You poor thing.' She examined it in detail. 'It looks nasty.'

'You should see it without make-up. It took all my skills to get it like this.'

Jenna whistled. 'And that's why you're the best in the biz.'

As Jenna guided them using Google Maps, they chatted about the morning they had ahead of them and soon they pulled up outside the address they'd been given.

They went into the kitchen, which seemed to be the hub of the home, and discovered that the house was teeming with the bride's family. Sisters, brothers, cousins, aunts and friends bustled in and out. The father of the bride was pacing around the kitchen, stressing about his speech and his wife was trying to force-feed everyone burnt sausages. Even though it was chaos, Lucy could feel that there was so much love and warmth in this little kitchen. The bride had three sisters and they all joked and teased one another with stories from when they were kids. Lucy loved listening to the banter between them; having only had brothers, she'd always wanted a sister. She loved the idea of a big, busy family like this, everyone rushing around. It was exactly like what she had grown up with. She automatically found herself thinking about Anabel growing up as an only child; who would rally around her on the morning of her wedding? It would be a pretty sedate affair if it was just herself, Anabel and Neil, that was for sure. She pushed the thoughts from her head as the first of the bridesmaids, the bride's older sister Karen, sat down in the chair in front of her and she set to work on her face.

'You were in the wars,' Karen remarked, nodding at the bruise above Lucy's eye in the mirror.

Lucy nodded as she blended the primer into the woman's skin.

'What happened to you?' she continued.

'I slipped in the kitchen and banged my face off the island.' Even though it was the truth – she had slipped – Lucy could hear a pinch in her voice as she told the woman what had happened.

'Here's your clumsy sister.' Karen stabbed herself with her index finger. 'Sure, one time I fell down the stairs – like I somehow managed to roll the whole way from the top step right to the bottom and hit every one on the way down. You should have seen the state of my face after it. Poor Pete was mortified; he said that everyone would think he had done it.' Karen threw her head back and laughed heartily.

'Well, I don't feel so bad now after hearing that. What are we like?' Lucy laughed along, but it didn't explain the seedy feeling sitting in her tummy as she chatted with the woman. Why did she feel embarrassed about it all? Neil had said it had been an accident. That's what had happened. She had to keep telling herself that because the alternative... well, she didn't want to think about that.

Everyone thought they were the perfect couple. Her friends said they were love's young dream. Teenage sweethearts, they had been inseparable since they'd met in school. Neil had sat beside her in geography class on the first day of second year. They had only been fourteen. He always made her laugh and soon they started going out. He had been her first and only boyfriend. They finished school and even though her parents had aspirations for her to go to university, she and Neil had both decided to get jobs and start saving to move in together. *You're a smart girl,* they'd said. *You could be the first in our family to get a degree,* but Lucy was adamant that she wanted to start earning money.

She knew they wanted more for her than what they had had, always renting, trying to stretch out their wages until payday, always struggling to make ends meet, but Lucy told them that she and Neil were different. And they were. She got an office job answering phones and Neil sold cars in a dealership. She did a make-up artist course by night and then started helping out with wedding parties on weekends. She developed a reputation in the bridal industry and soon was able to ditch her office job and go freelance as a make-up artist. Neil then got mad into working out and decided to become a personal trainer. He worked in a gym for a few years before opening his own place. Although she'd never say it to her parents, she was proud of them for being ambitious and proving everyone wrong. They hadn't gone the traditional route, but they had made a success of their lives, despite her parents' concerns about not going to university. They'd got married when they were twenty-three, then had Anabel soon after. They had worked hard, saved like mad to get on the property ladder and then had finally saved enough to buy number 28, St Brigid's Road.

Lucy always thought their story so romantic: starry-eyed young lovers who, despite everyone telling them that they were too young, had made a success of their lives. How, against all the odds, they had made it work because love trumped everything. She could imagine Anabel telling her own children about their great love story some day and getting swept up in the romance of it all. That was why she had to believe him. She didn't want their perfect life tainted. She just needed the bruising to fade and then she could put the whole sorry mess behind her.

7

When Lucy came home that evening she was met by the smell of her favourite dinner; Neil was cooking a Thai red curry with prawns. He always made the curry paste himself from scratch; he complained that it took ages to do it, but they both agreed it tasted so much better than shop-bought pastes. It was normally a dish he would cook at the weekends when they had more time to spend chopping chillies and blending spices, so she knew if he was cooking it on a midweek evening it must be because he was feeling guilty.

Neil had collected Anabel from the after-school service, and she was glued to the TV, barely registering her mother coming in the door. As Lucy took off her coat, she watched Neil flinch when he saw the bruising around her eye. She wasn't sure if she was imagining it, but she swore his face was washed with shame. It had all happened so fast; one minute she had been walking across the floor and the next she had heard his footsteps behind her and was careering down towards the island, seeing the quartz countertop coming up to greet her. She'd wanted to believe what Neil had said about her having slipped, but now, as she looked into his guilty eyes, she knew there had been nothing wrong with that floor.

You see, this wasn't the first time something like this had happened, and it hadn't felt right then either. She used to have a big gang of girlfriends before she had got married but she rarely saw them now. They were all busy with their own lives and she was a mum now too while they were still childless, so she wasn't as carefree as they were. They had all been down in the pub for Julie's twenty-first birthday, including her and Neil. Julie had suggested that they should go on a girly weekend away together that summer. They had been excitedly making plans about where they would go. *Ibiza*, someone suggested; *London*, someone else said. In the taxi that night, Neil was silent the whole way home. When they got back to their apartment, she had asked him what was wrong. He had ignored her. She thought he'd had too much to drink – he didn't usually drink much; he didn't like losing control, he said that one of them needed to be aware of their surroundings – but that night he had been in a round with the other lads and she knew he had drunk a lot more than he usually would.

She had been getting into her pyjamas, when suddenly she'd felt his arms grab her from behind. With his top lip pared back, exposing his gritted teeth, he had pinned her to the wall with his hand around her throat and his contorted face had hurled abuse at her. As she had desperately searched out air in the room, he'd told her that she was a stupid whore, and that there was no way he was letting her go away for a holiday with a group of slags. He told her he knew what happened on these weekends away – that it was an excuse to sleep with other guys. He said he never went anywhere with his friends, so why should she go away with hers for a weekend? It was true, Neil didn't really have many friends; his friends were the boyfriends of her friends.

She had tried so hard to breathe but he was choking her, his grip getting ever tighter until she couldn't seem to pull air into her lungs. She began to panic. Eventually, when she'd thought she was going to pass out, he had let her go. As she collapsed onto the bed, taking great, heaving gulps of air into her lungs, he was already apologising profusely. He blamed the drink – he had been trying to keep up with the lads. He had been so sorry afterwards; he had even cried. In the end, she had felt sorry for him; she hated seeing him so weighed down with remorse.

There was another time too, when Annie had only been a baby; they had had an argument over whose turn it was to get up to her during the night. Neil had already been up to put in her soother, but when she had woken a second time, Lucy hadn't heard her cry, so Neil had got up again. Lucy had woken then and followed him into Anabel's nursery, but he had pushed her out of the way. She had stumbled backwards and hit her head on the wall. The next day he had claimed she had tripped over a toy left lying on the floor, but she knew she hadn't. That time she had blamed it on the sleep deprivation that came with having an infant.

Those incidents had been a long time ago but the seedy feeling she had experienced then was the same: the uncertainty and confusion over what had actually happened, and the way Neil could spin things around to make her doubt her version of events. He had never hit her. That was the thing. Over the years there had been the odd push and sometimes his temper and sheer physical strength scared her, but he had never hit her.

'How was your day?' he asked, not meeting her eyes.

'I've had better,' she admitted, placing her handbag down on the island.

He moved towards her and reached out to caress her face. 'Your poor face.'

She pulled away from him.

'Don't be like that with me, Lu; you know it was an accident.'

'Was it?' she challenged, surprising herself. Where had that come from?

He looked shocked. 'You slipped, Lucy,' he said firmly. 'You know that. I promise – on Annie's life – that I'd never hurt you.'

She nodded, suddenly feeling so exhausted by it all and not wishing to argue any more. There was no point dragging this on. She couldn't remember exactly what had happened. She hated when they argued. She wanted to forget about it too.

'I know,' she sighed.

He slipped his arm around her waist and this time she didn't move away from his touch.

'I'm sorry,' he said once again; his fingers found hers and he gave her hand a squeeze.

She let herself relax in his embrace. This was what their marriage was like; it could be stormy, but they loved one another. The fabric that joined them together was bigger than this. She knew she just had to wait out the simmering tension and then like a squall that had blown itself out, things would eventually be calm once more. The sun would be shining between them again and they would forget all about it.

8

A few days later, I was just settling down to watch *Judge Judy* when I heard Dora whine from the hall. I put my tea down and dragged myself up from the chair. I followed her out and found her sitting at the door. She cocked her head at me and gave another whimper.

'Do you need to go out, love?' I asked.

Immediately, she wagged her stubby little tail. I swear to God that dog understood everything I said to her. I took her lead off the newel post of the stairs and opened the door but before I could clip it to her collar, she had scurried out ahead of me. She didn't even give me time to put my coat on. 'Oh no you don't, Dora Murphy!' I said, hurrying after her. If she did her business next door again, I'd never hear the end of it. 'Get back here, you cheeky bugger!' I called.

I followed her out into the fading light of the day. The days were so short at this time of year, it was almost dark, and it was only four thirty.

'Dora!' I heard a voice cry. I looked over the wall next door and saw Anabel was playing on her scooter on the driveway. She was still in her school uniform but the neat plaits that she had been sporting when I had watched her from my window as she was going to school with her mum earlier that morning were now askew and loose strands of hair had come undone around her face. She threw down the scooter, came over to the wall and immediately Dora's tail started to pulse from side to side.

'Can I come and say hi to Dora?' she begged.

'Well...' I said hesitantly. 'I think you should ask your mammy if it's okay. She might not like you wandering off.' The last thing I wanted was the child getting into trouble.

'She won't know,' Anabel said brazenly, using her two arms to hoist herself up as she climbed over the wall.

'Be careful,' I warned as she jumped down on to my side.

'Hi, Dora,' Anabel said as she landed on the grass.

She bent down on her hunkers and let Dora climb up onto her knees.

'Mind she doesn't put hairs all over your uniform,' I said.

'I don't care if she does.' She giggled as Dora licked her hand.

'You might not care but your mammy might,' I retorted.

'What's your name?' she asked, ignoring me.

'I'm Eileen.'

'Eileen,' she repeated thoughtfully. 'What age is Dora?'

'I'm not sure; she was a stray.'

'What does that mean?'

'It's when a dog doesn't have an owner.'

'So how did you get to be her owner then?'

'Well, she just turned up on my doorstep, so she didn't give me much choice.'

'You're lucky. I wish she came to my house. I want a dog, but my daddy doesn't like them. He says they put shit and hair everywhere. I know shit is a bad word,' she added, 'but that's what Daddy always says.'

I grimaced. Yet another reason to dislike Mr Muscle. 'Well, Dora is a very tidy little dog,' I said, jumping to Dora's defence.

Anabel continued making a big fuss of Dora when

suddenly I heard a door open.

'Anabel! What are you doing over there?' Lucy's voice shouted. 'Get back here. I told you that if you want to play on your scooter that you're not allowed to leave our driveway!'

'Uh-oh,' Anabel said, springing up from the ground. 'I'm coming, Mammy.'

Lucy's high heels clacked across their driveway as she approached the wall and waited for Anabel to return. Who wore high heels around the house? She had a full face of make-up on and her long blonde hair fell in soft waves down her back. The black eye had faded now and was barely noticeable underneath all the make-up. She was always so glamorous, I wondered if she ever let herself go without the warpaint or without having her hair coiffed. Everything about my neighbours seemed styled to perfection; their home, their clothes, their cars – everything was immaculate and flawless. She threw a hasty 'hello' in my direction before turning to her daughter. As Lucy waited for Anabel to come back around to their side, I could tell by the pinch in her face and the way she wouldn't meet my gaze that she didn't want to get drawn into conversation with me. I knew Lucy probably saw me as their odd next-door neighbour. Maybe she even thought I was a bit cuckoo. She didn't know the woman I had once been before, the busy mother just like her with a beautiful home and a family to love.

'Don't ever do that again, do you hear me?' I could hear Lucy scolding the child all the way back into their house. 'You know you're not allowed talk to strangers. How many times do I have to tell you?'

'She's not a stranger; her name is Eileen.'

'Stop being cheeky!'

'But she's our neighbour and you always say that we have to be friendly to our neighbours,' Anabel protested.

I had a giggle at that. She was smart one, that child.

'That's enough, Anabel!' Lucy warned, tugging on her hand.

'I was only saying hi to Dora.' Anabel began to cry as Lucy marched her inside. The door slammed, causing me to jump.

I looked down at Dora who was sitting looking up at me with her head tilted to the side, confused about what had just happened. She looked disappointed as her playmate disappeared inside the house. 'Well now, Miss Dora,' I tutted as I shook my head at the terrier. 'You're after getting the poor child into trouble.'

9

The next day, Lucy pulled the front door closed behind her and led Anabel towards the car.

'Come on, Annie, love,' she said, ushering her daughter down the driveway. She held the door open and waited for her to climb into the back seat. 'We don't want to be late.'

She noticed a shadow lurking behind the net curtain next door. The woman from next door, who she now knew was called Eileen, was watching them again. It was the same thing every morning: she would be standing at the side of the window, peering out at them through her net curtains or sometimes she would even be in her garden pretending to be putting out the bins or bringing the dog to the toilet. She was always looking at them coming and going. Eileen seemed to have no friends or family; Lucy had never seen anyone call there bar the postman. The only time she left the house was to bring her little dog for a walk. She didn't appear to have a job and Lucy didn't know how she survived financially. She almost felt sorry for the woman who clearly had nothing better to do with her life. Lucy had mentioned it to Neil, and he said she did the same to him when he was leaving for work and that it was really creeping him out. Neil reckoned she was raking in the benefits. He would point towards her house. 'That's our taxes keeping Mad Mary in that house,' he would say. 'You and me working our arses off to pay for her to live on this road and then she hasn't even the decency to keep it looking nice.' For some reason that Lucy couldn't fathom, Anabel seemed to be taken with her. If the woman was out in the garden with the dog, Annie would ask if she could pet it and if she saw Eileen standing at the side of the window, with her net curtain twitching, she would give her a wave.

Lucy looked away from Eileen's tatty house and helped Anabel into the car, then they set off for the school. That morning Lucy was booked to do a photo shoot for a bridal magazine. She was really excited about it. She had never done a photo shoot before, and she figured she would be allowed some more creative licence than she usually would get away with on her brides. She would also be credited in the magazine too so she hoped it would be a good advertisement for her business.

The shoot was taking place in a warehouse in the city centre, and she had arranged to meet Jenna there. When she arrived at the location, she climbed a concrete staircase and entered a vast open-plan space with exposed stone walls and raw steel beams. After the director had talked them through the different styles and the look she hoped to achieve, they set to work.

Lucy was just finishing off her third model when she began to feel dizzy. She guessed it was low blood sugar; she had been too busy to eat and had only grabbed a banana from the catering that had been brought in at lunchtime.

'Are you okay?' Jenna asked, eyeing her up as she collapsed into a chair after she had finished with the model and had sat down to take a breather. 'You're looking a little peaky.'

'I'm feeling a little light-headed,' Lucy admitted.

'Why don't you take five? We've only one model left, and I can do her. The stylist doesn't want anything too dramatic anyway for this look, so it won't take me long.'

'Are you sure?' Lucy asked.

'Of course. Go grab yourself a snack and hopefully you'll feel better then.'

'Thanks, Jenna, you're a star.'

Lucy felt a rush of gratitude towards her friend. As she stood up, a wave of dizziness almost floored her. Using the wall to steady herself, she made her way to the back of the room where she had left her bag. She rooted around inside and thankfully found a bar of chocolate in there. Sitting down in a chair, Lucy opened the wrapper, broke off a square and popped it into her mouth, waiting for the sugar to kick in. After fifteen minutes she still wasn't feeling great. She was nauseous and felt as though she'd had a wild night out. She hoped she wasn't coming down with something; she had a full diary for the next few weeks, and she couldn't afford to be sick. Maybe she was getting her period. She fished her phone out of her bag and checked her Health app to see when it was due. As she looked at the calendar, she realised that her period was late, and it was never late. Stunned, she put the phone in her bag and zipped it back up. Could she be? Surely not... A warm fizzing bubbled up inside her at the very idea. She remembered then that she'd woken up ravenous during the night. She had had to go downstairs and eat a bowl of cereal. This was exactly how she had felt during the early weeks of her pregnancy with Anabel. But how could she be pregnant? She was on the pill; Neil insisted on it. She didn't want to get her hopes up because realistically she knew the chances of her being pregnant were slim, but she still wondered *what if*? How many times had she heard stories about women falling pregnant on the pill and they had no idea how it had happened? She couldn't help but get carried away by the idea that she might be pregnant. She knew she wasn't going to persuade Neil to try for another baby any time soon so a part of her longed for an accident. Oh, but it would be a happy accident. She allowed herself to play out the fantasy for a moment. Anabel stroking the taut skin of her rounded belly and talking to the bump. Anabel leading a wobbling, pudgy-handed baby down the garden path as it learnt to walk. Although she knew Neil wouldn't be pleased initially if she was pregnant, he would come around. No one ever regretted their children even when they were unplanned.

'How are you feeling now?' Jenna came into the room a while later, pulling her out of her thoughts. Her friend's face was creased in concern.

'A little better,' Lucy said. It was the truth; somehow the idea that she might be pregnant had made her feel a little brighter and her peakiness seemed to have disappeared. 'I found some chocolate in my bag, and it seems to have done the trick.' She smiled at Jenna.

'Chocolate is the best medicine,' Jenna agreed. 'Well, we're all finished with the models. I'm just going to tidy up and then we're done.'

'Thanks, Jenna. You're a star.' She pulled herself up and returned to the area they had been working in, keen to get finished up and go home. She had decided to stop in a pharmacy on her way and buy a pregnancy test just in case. She was teasing herself with these thoughts. Even though she knew it was probably wishful thinking, she needed to know for sure.

10

Lucy emerged from the pharmacy and placed the paper bag containing the pregnancy test on the passenger seat beside her. As the traffic stalled and started the whole way home, she longed to be able to find out the answer right then and put herself out of her misery.

She was finished early enough that she could collect Anabel from the after-school service. Anabel's face lit up when she saw her mum standing at the school gate to collect her; it was normally her father who picked her up. She ran over and threw her arms around her. Lucy's heart swelled inside her chest. Being a mum was the best thing that had ever happened to her. How amazing it would be to give Anabel a sibling. She looked around her at the other parents standing at the school gate waiting to collect their children: some had buggies with toddlers strapped in, others held the hands of preschool-aged children. She watched a little boy emerge from the school building and run across the yard to hug his little brother. He then showed him a picture he had drawn in school. She wanted that for Anabel. She wanted her to have a baby brother or sister to love and to tell them all about what she had done in school that day.

As they drove from the school through the suburban streets, she let her mind drift off on a fantasy where she was telling Anabel that she was pregnant, and the child was overjoyed.

When they got home, she chopped up some apple segments for Anabel and then headed straight upstairs to the bathroom. She had planned on waiting until her daughter was in bed later that evening, but she couldn't help herself. The suspense was killing her; she needed to know now whether she was pregnant or not. She took the test out of the box and unfolded the leaflet inside. She quickly scanned the instructions and then held the stick under her urine. She left it on the side of the bathtub while she timed it on her watch. She stared at the stick as the liquid seeped across the panel and the control line turned pink. It seemed to take an eternity. She busied around the bathroom, tidying up her cosmetics. Neil was always moaning that she left her make-up thrown around. She checked her watch and saw the two minutes was up. She held her breath as she picked the test up from where she had left it on the bathtub and examined it closely. There was only one line. She studied it hard for even the faintest hint of a second line, but there was nothing there, not even a trace. The panel was stark white. She wasn't pregnant. Why had she been so stupid to get her hopes up? She had known that it was highly unlikely. She put the test in the bin, buried her disappointment and came back downstairs to Anabel.

She returned to the kitchen and looked around for her daughter, but she didn't see her. She moved closer to her play area and peeped over the bank of toy storage that divided it from the living room, but she wasn't there either. She turned and looked around the living area again. Where on earth could she be?

'Annie?' she called out but there was no reply.

She came back out and ran up the stairs, taking the steps two at a time. She checked Anabel's bedroom but there was no sign of her. She came down again, calling her daughter's name.

'Anabel, if you're hiding on me, Mammy is going

to be very cross with you,' she warned. This wasn't the time for hide-and-seek.

She returned to the kitchen and checked again, but Anabel definitely wasn't in there. Normally, she asked if she wanted to play outside on her scooter and Lucy would keep watch on her through the front window. They lived on a busy road; if Anabel wandered on to the street, she could be killed. She opened the front door and ran outside into the dark evening, calling the child's name.

'Anabel? Are you out here, Anabel?' She searched around for her daughter, her eyes trying to adjust to the dim street lighting. The air was thick with woodsmoke from the nearby chimneys and it scratched her throat. She peered through the darkness but there was no sign of her. Then she felt the presence. There was someone else there. She could feel them watching her through the velvety blackness of the evening.

'She's over here,' a gravelly voice said suddenly, causing Lucy to scream with fright.

She turned in the direction of the voice and saw Eileen from next door was standing in the shadows looking across at her.

Lucy peered through the darkness and spotted Anabel crouched down on the weedy grass beside her, petting the dog. Relief, warm and joyous, washed through her but was quickly replaced by anger.

'Anabel! What are you doing over there?' Lucy scolded, approaching the wall that separated their houses. 'Get back here. I already told you yesterday that you are not allowed to wander off. I was worried about you.'

Anabel jumped up. 'I'm coming, Mammy.'

'She was only saying hi to Dora,' Eileen replied, coming to Anabel's defence, her tone barely concealing the fact that she felt Lucy was overreacting.

Lucy felt her temper flare. Who did this woman think she was? How dare she! Did she know how worried Lucy had been? This woman knew nothing about children and trying to keep them safe with the ever-present dangers of today's world. 'She's not allowed to leave our driveway, she knows that.' Lucy stood defiant.

Anabel returned to their own drive and, without meeting Eileen's eyes, Lucy took her daughter by the hand and led her back into the house.

'Don't ever do that again, do you hear me?' she scolded the child as they went inside. 'You're not allowed go outside without my permission.'

'I just wanted to rub Dora.' Anabel began to cry and guilt floored Lucy; she knew she was overreacting, but Anabel had given her a fright. That coupled with the disappointment of not being pregnant had caused her to snap, but she shouldn't have taken her stress out on the child.

'I'm sorry, love, I was worried, that's all,' she explained, her tone softer now. 'Let's go back inside and have a nice hot chocolate.' She forced herself to sound bright for Anabel's sake even though her heart was pierced with the bitter tang of disappointment.

Anabel reached up and slotted her hand inside her own, her upset quickly forgotten and Lucy knew she had been forgiven. Her daughter's unconditional love for her broke her even more. As she led the child down the hallway, Anabel's soft hand trusting inside her own, she berated herself. What was wrong with her? Why couldn't she be happy with her lot? She had everything she had ever wanted and more – a lovely family and home – so why couldn't she just be happy with that? Why did she need another child? She had the most perfect daughter, a great husband, and their dream house. She had everything she wanted right here; she needed to cop herself on.

11

Lucy was still fuming with Eileen as she boiled the milk on the hob to make the hot chocolate for Anabel. She always seemed to be there, watching them, her beady eyes following them around their own home, and now she seemed to have befriended Anabel. It was unnerving. Lucy needed to keep an eye on that situation; they didn't know anything about the woman. For all they knew, she could be unhinged.

A short time later she saw the two yellow beams of Neil's headlights in the driveway. She knew by the slam of the front door as he came into the house and the way his feet pounded over the floor that he wasn't in a good mood.

'How was your day?' she asked, but she could tell by the set of his jaw and the way his shoulders were hiked that it clearly hadn't gone well. They were just starting to get back on a better footing after their last argument and she didn't want to upset things between them again.

He mumbled something at her as he put his gear bag into the cloakroom.

'Annie is making Play-Doh cupcakes. She tried to force-feed me one,' she whispered, thumbing over to where Anabel was playing in her toy kitchen.

He ignored her and moved brusquely around the room and when Anabel tried to get him to eat a cupcake, he didn't even attempt to feign interest. She watched their daughter retreating back to her play area, her whole body sagging in defeat. Lucy felt herself flood with disappointment for the second time that day. Couldn't he just play along for Anabel's sake?

'What is it? What's wrong?' she asked eventually, growing impatient with his sulking. He was moodier than the sea on a winter's day; he had changed the whole atmosphere of the house since he'd walked through the door. She hadn't had a great day either, all things considered. She was crushed with disappointment, but she had the good sense to know she needed to forget about it and plaster a smile on her face for the sake of her family.

'Nothing...' he retorted.

'It can't be nothing; I can see that you've got something on your mind.'

'Will you just leave me alone, for God's sakes,' he snapped. 'You're always at me, yakking on, wrecking my head about everything.'

'Sorry I seem to be annoying you so much lately,' she said bitterly. She felt tears prick her eyes. *Damn it*, she didn't want Anabel to see her upset. She went upstairs to the bathroom and used toilet roll to dry her tears. She sat down on the edge of the bathtub and opened the bin where she had stuffed the test earlier. She knew it was wishful thinking, but she had heard of lines developing several hours later. She studied it but the panel was still chalk white where she had hoped for a second line. Suddenly, the door burst open behind her, startling her. The test fell out of her hands and on to the floor. She swung around and saw Neil standing there.

'What was that?' he said. 'What are you doing?'

'Nothing.' She moved to stand in front of where it lay on the tiles.

'What is that?' He pointed to the stick lying beside her feet.

'It's a pregnancy test,' she confessed, feeling embarrassed that she had let herself get carried away with the idea that she might be pregnant even though it was virtually impossible. He would think she was stupid and probably berate her for wasting their money.

He bent to pick it up and examined it. His brows pinched together as his whole face clouded over. 'Why would you have to do a pregnancy test?'

She shrugged. 'I just thought I might be...'

'But how could you be pregnant?' He blinked rapidly. 'You're on the pill.'

She splayed her arms. 'I know, it was ridiculous of me... but my period was late, and I was feeling a bit off. I guess... I kind of hoped that maybe I might be...'

Suddenly, his eyes darkened, and heat crept up his face. 'Did you stop taking your pill, Lucy? Because that's the only way you could be pregnant.'

'Of course not!' She was insulted.

He took a step forward, closing the space between them. 'You better be telling me the truth. Are you still on the pill?' he repeated through gritted teeth.

'I-I swear to you I am,' she said quickly, praying that he would believe her.

'Well then, why are you doing a test?'

'Because I really want another baby, Neil.'

'Why won't you listen to me? We can't afford another baby. Why won't you get that into your head?' he shouted.

Suddenly, she felt herself being pulled by her hair; he was holding it tightly, wrapped around his fist. 'When are you going to realise? We won't be having another baby. Not ever.'

'Stop it, Neil,' she gasped. 'You're hurting me. Let go.'

'Who are you sleeping with?' he snarled, pulling tighter so that she thought her hair was going to be yanked from her head. He lowered his face so that he was only inches from hers. His teeth were bared like a vicious dog, and it looked as though he hated her. He probably hated how stupid she was.

'Please let go, you're hurting me,' she whimpered.

'You're a stupid slut!' he roared, then his other hand reached out and slammed into the side of her face. Before she knew what was happening, he let go of her hair and shoved her, so she was falling to the floor. Her head hit the tiles with an almighty thwack.

Then there was a ferocious pain in her ribs, followed swiftly by another one, and she realised he was kicking her. His foot kept making contact, each kick more powerful than the last until her ribs were on fire and she couldn't draw breath into her lungs.

'Daddy, Daddy, what are you doing?' she heard Anabel's voice cry out. 'Stop it! *Please, Daddy!*' was the last thing she heard just before everything went black.

12

Someone was crying. She recognised the sound. It was a child. There was a child crying. She realised it was coming from Anabel. Anabel was crying. She felt her chest tighten. It was so hard to breathe. Every intake of breath felt as though shards of broken glass were being inhaled into her lungs. A dog was barking too and a voice that wasn't familiar to her was calling her name.

'Lucy, love, can you hear me?' the voice asked again.

She took a moment to get her bearings, straining to make out the different sounds before trying to open her eyes, but only one of them moved. The room was circling around her as if she was sitting on a spinning top.

'Take it easy now, there you go,' the voice soothed. 'It's Eileen from next door. Are you okay?'

She tried to nod but her neck throbbed from the movement. Her vision steadied and she saw the woman come into focus. Eileen was kneeling beside her on the floor, crouched over her. What was she doing here? Lucy tried to lift her head slightly and saw Anabel standing in the door frame with the woman's dog yapping in her arms.

Panic suffocated her. *Where was he now?* If Neil saw Eileen and that dog here, who knew what he'd do. 'You have to go,' Lucy warned. 'Please, just go—'

'Don't worry, he's not here,' Eileen said as if she had read her mind.

Eileen turned to the barking dog in Anabel's arms.

'Would you give it over, Dora?' she sighed. 'I already told you; he's gone now.' The dog whimpered before falling quiet.

Why were they all in her bathroom? Lucy wondered. She caught sight of the pregnancy test lying on the tiles and the events of that evening came rushing back and engulfed her like a tidal wave. The horrible accusations. The sudden punch to her face that seemed to come from nowhere. Neil kicking her with such brutal force that she had honestly thought she was going to die. She raised her hand to touch her head and felt her hair was sticky with blood.

Lucy looked at the wall beside her and saw the lovely soft-grey subway tiles that they had spent ages deciding over were now smeared with her blood. A headache was thumping against her skull. But it was Anabel's face that frightened her the most. The poor child looked petrified; tears shone in her petrol-blue eyes.

'It's okay, Anabel,' she said. She tried once again to manoeuvre herself up from the floor, but she was too weak.

'I'll give you a hand,' Eileen said, putting her hands beneath her armpits and helping to lift her. She guided her out of the bathroom. 'Well, it doesn't look like anything is broken,' she said as she sat her down on the side of the bed. Anabel placed the dog down on the floor and climbed up onto the bed, throwing her arms around her.

'Mammy, I was so scared,' she hiccupped. Lucy felt her daughter's tears come hot and furious against her neck.

'I'm so sorry, Anabel.' She began to cry with her as the events of that evening caught up with her.

'What happened?' Eileen asked, once she had

made her comfortable on the bed.

'I-I think I must have fallen...' Lucy lied.

'You just fell over in the bathroom and hit your head on the tiles, huh?' Eileen's tone was heavy with sarcasm and Lucy felt mortified that Eileen could see through her so easily.

'No, Mammy,' Anabel said shaking her head. 'You didn't fall. Daddy didded it. He kicked you, Mammy.'

'No, Anabel, Daddy didn't do it,' she said firmly. She needed to protect Anabel from this. Anabel didn't need to know that sometimes her daddy could be a monster and if that meant denying the truth then that was what she had to do.

'But he did, Mammy!' Anabel insisted. 'I saw him do it!'

'Shh, Anabel,' Lucy said more firmly this time, and the child began to cry again.

'It's okay, Anabel,' Eileen said, smiling sympathetically at the child. She had kind eyes, Lucy thought. She hadn't noticed that before.

Eileen went into the bathroom and came back with damp cotton wool which she used to clean up her eye. While Eileen tended to her, Lucy began shivering uncontrollably; her arms and legs were shaking, even her teeth chattered together.

'It's the shock,' Eileen said, removing the faux fur

throw that was draped over the end of the bed and placing it around her shoulders. 'I'll go down and make you a cuppa. It's all going to be okay.'

Lucy nodded gratefully. She wasn't sure how the woman from next door had got into her house, but she didn't care; she was thankful that she had come when she had. She didn't know what might have happened if she hadn't... Would he have kept pummelling her? *Would he have killed her?* When she'd been crouched on the floor in the foetal position with her hands over her head as he had kicked every last breath of air out of her lungs, it had certainly felt that way. She had been terrified, and the worst part of it all wasn't the violence, it was that Anabel had witnessed the whole thing. She couldn't hide the truth from Anabel any longer. Their daughter had seen it with her own eyes that her daddy wasn't the man she thought he was. Lucy had tried so hard to protect her from it, but she had failed, and now this would mar her childhood forever more.

The little dog followed Eileen downstairs and, while they were gone, she pulled her daughter in tight against her chest, and even though every bone in her ribcage hurt, she didn't care; she needed to feel Anabel close to her. She wanted Anabel to know that she was safe and secure even though she wasn't sure if that was true any more.

13

I let myself in the door to number 26 with Dora right by my heels. Her nails clacked on the floorboards behind me as I headed straight to the kitchen. I flicked the switch on the kettle, turned and rested my back against the Formica countertop and looked down at the little dog. 'Well, Dora, what did you think of that, eh?' I asked as the kettle came to life.

Dora pricked her ears, cocked her head to the side and gave a whine in response.

'I know, love, I know,' I sighed. 'Hardly the best evening we've had, was it?' I bent down and scratched her.

My eyes fell on the bottle of wine that Theo and Chris from number 30 had dropped in when I had

moved in earlier in the year. It was still sitting in the
sparkly gift bag that they had presented me with.
That had been an awkward encounter. They had arrived at my door in a flurry of excitement on the day I
had moved in. Tim had only just left, when the bell
had rung. At first, I had been too scared to open the
door, but they had pushed open the letter box calling,
'Yoo-hoo, it's your new neighbours, we just want to welcome you to St Brigid's Road.' Reluctantly, I had opened
the door and found the two of them standing there
on the step, full of the joys. They had introduced
themselves and then enthusiastically welcomed me
to St Brigid's Road. The more I had stayed silent, the
more they had gushed about how wonderful the area
was, telling me when bin day was and giving tips
about the best broadband provider. Eventually, I had
taken the bottle from them and closed the door
without inviting them in. Had I even thanked them
for the wine? Probably not. I reached out, lifted the
bottle of Pinot Noir from the bag and traced my
finger over the raised print on the label. Lord knows I
could have used something a bit stronger than tea
after everything that had happened that evening. The
noise of the child's screams split with Dora's incessant
barking was still ringing in my ears. I placed the
bottle down again on the counter. I was doing so well

these days; I didn't want to risk slipping back into my old ways.

When the doorbell had rung earlier that evening, I had been planning on ignoring it. I had just washed up after dinner and made myself cosy in front of the fire. I thought it was probably some politician wanting to give me his spiel for the local elections and I had no time for any of that lark. But the bell had been pressed again and then again a second later in a stop-start, jagged manner. I guessed it was some of the children on the road playing knick-knacks. After the fifth time, I was beginning to lose patience. In my day, you did it once and ran away. I had turned to Dora. 'Do they think I've nothing better to be doing than listening to that carry on?'

'Right, that's it!' I announced when it sounded again. 'I've had enough.' I stood up and headed for the door. Dora jumped up after me, her nails clacking along the floorboards. When I looked through the spyglass, there was no one there. I turned and was about to go back to the sitting room when the bell rang again. I took the chain off the door and opened it to see little Anabel standing on my doorstep. Her small face looked distraught.

'Are you okay, love?' I asked, looking around her to see if her parents were nearby.

Anabel shook her head. 'My mammy won't wake up. Daddy hurt her.' She reached out and tugged on my hand. 'Please, you have to come, Eileen,' she begged with her bottom lip trembling.

Without thinking twice, I followed Anabel down my own drive and up the resin-bound driveway next door with Dora trailing after us. At the same time Mr Muscle's car was backing out and I quickly pulled Anabel out of the way before he reversed over her. I caught a glimpse of him through the windscreen. He was so clouded with anger that he didn't seem to notice us. I felt fear flood through me. What the hell was going on? I hurried into the house after Anabel.

'She's upstairs,' Anabel said as she began climbing the steps. Dora began to bark as she followed us up.

I ran up the stairs after Anabel, wondering what awaited me, knowing that whatever it was, it wouldn't be good. Anabel made her way towards the front bedroom and then into the small en-suite bathroom where we found Lucy lying slumped on the floor. Orangey-red blood was smeared across the tiles at the back of her head. Icy sweat broke out all along my neck. I was pretty sure that Lucy was dead. Dora whined uneasily and started barking again. What had he done to her? I bent down on my hunkers beside Lucy, checking for a pulse and calling her name.

'Is my mammy okay?' Anabel asked.

'Of course she is,' I lied, because what else could I tell the child?

Eventually, Lucy's eyes started to flicker and gradually she opened them. I said a Hail Mary in relief.

'Take it easy now, there you go,' I soothed as she came round. 'I'm Eileen from next door. Are you okay?'

Anabel was watching us from the doorway and every now and then a tiny sob would choke in her throat.

'It's all going to be okay, Anabel,' I reassured her. She had picked Dora up and was hugging her in her arms.

I guided Lucy up off the floor and out of the poky bathroom. Thankfully, she was able to walk. Her arms seemed to be working okay and she didn't appear to have any broken bones. Her face was a different story, however. Her right eye was swollen and closed over. It was already starting to bruise, and it would be a right mess tomorrow. She was barely recognisable from the glamourous young woman who I watched through the window as she sashayed down the driveway every morning. Mr Muscle had done a right job on her, so he had. Anabel put Dora down and climbed up on the bed to cuddle her mother.

I returned to the bathroom and found a bag of cotton wool balls in the en suite and tended to Lucy's eye. This time he'd managed to batter the opposite side of her face. Poor Lucy started shivering violently then as the shock took over. I went downstairs and made a cup of tea for her, nearly pouring half a bag of sugar into the mug to help with the shock. I located the freezer, took out a bag of peas and wrapped them in a towel. When I came back upstairs, I instructed Lucy to hold it up to the nasty swelling above her eye. She was in a right sorry state as she sat on the bed holding the peas up to her forehead with one hand, and the other clutching her tea.

Anabel eventually fell asleep, curled up beside her mother. I covered her with the duvet and Dora sat protectively on the floor at her bedside. I swore that dog had a sixth sense when it came to people needing help. Lucy was stroking her daughter's hair which was stuck to her tear-stained face. God love her. I hated seeing the child like this. She was an adorable, friendly little thing and I had grown fond of her. Her little smile could light my heart for hours. Dora liked her too and she was a good judge of character. I found myself going outside when I saw them leaving the house, just so I could see her. I'd pretend I was putting out the bins or bringing Dora to the toilet so I could say hi to her. Sometimes Anabel's smile or her little wave over the wall as her parents led her to the car was the only little bit of joy in my whole day.

'What happened tonight?' I tried again. Now that Anabel was asleep, I hoped that Lucy might open up to me.

'I fell...'

'Did your husband do this to you?' I asked even though I knew full well it was his fault – Anabel had told me the same. The last time I had seen Lucy with a shiner, I hadn't known what had happened, but this time I knew the truth.

Lucy shook her head. 'Of course not. I told you: I fell. Anabel was just confused about what she saw.'

'All right,' I said, not wanting to push it any more with her. I headed back into the bathroom, found a cloth in the cupboard under the sink and began wiping Lucy's blood off the tiles because I knew it would be distressing if she saw that mess later.

'Why don't you both stay with me tonight?' I suggested when I was finished cleaning the bathroom.

Lucy shook her head. 'We'll be okay here.'

'But what if he comes back and he's still angry?' I pleaded.

Lucy shook her head. 'I told you; this wasn't his fault.'

'Well, why don't you call your family then or a friend? Maybe one of them might stay over with you,' I suggested. I didn't want to leave them here alone to face Neil. Who knew what kind of a mood he'd be in whenever he returned?

'We'll be fine.' Lucy stood up then, indicating that she wanted me to go.

Stubborn that one, I thought. There was no helping some people. I knew when I wasn't wanted, and who could blame Lucy? We didn't know one another. She was in shock, the poor thing, without having me there in her bedroom gawping at her and making awkward conversation. I didn't want to be in this situation any more than she did, but circumstance had thrown us together and now we were both involved. I suspected that I knew more intimate details about Lucy than any of her family or closest friends. There wasn't much more I could do, so I said goodnight to Lucy and told her she was welcome next door at any time of the day or night. She nodded and thanked me.

As I made my way downstairs and back to my own house, I thought about calling the Gardaí and reporting what had happened, but I knew Lucy wouldn't appreciate me interfering like that. And besides, what could the Gardaí do anyway? I hadn't actually witnessed Mr Muscle lay a finger on her, so unless Lucy was willing to be honest about what had happened and press charges, there was nothing anyone could do, and it seemed she was still in denial.

I waited for the kettle to boil, made myself a cup of tea, then sat down in the armchair beside the window. I was terrified Neil might come back still crazy with rage, so I stayed up, keeping watch. I had drawn the curtains but left enough of a gap in the middle to peep through. It was after midnight when I eventually saw the orange glow of two headlights turn into the driveway next door. My heart began thumping like a wild bird trapped in a cage. I held my breath as he got out and made his way back into the house. Dora was snoring loudly beside me, and I prayed she wouldn't wake up and start barking all over again. I listened out as he went inside, but all seemed to be quiet between their four walls.

It was hard to believe that I had once looked in through their open curtains feeling a pang of jealousy for their perfect family. I had thought they had it all but what had happened tonight just proved that we all had skeletons in the closet; sometimes you just had to root around a little more to find them, but they were always there.

14

Lucy lay there, staring at the ceiling. The blood was pulsing in the wound above her eye as her mind kept replaying what had happened that evening. She was still in disbelief. She wished she could make excuses or tell herself that it had been another accident, but she couldn't deny it this time. There was no fudging it or pretending it hadn't happened, it was clear-cut: Neil had hit her and then just in case that hadn't been enough, he had kicked her repeatedly for good measure too, while their daughter looked on. Her own husband, the man who said he loved her, who rubbed her feet when they ached after a long day, who would fill a hot-water bottle when she had her period, the man with whom she shared her hopes and dreams, had turned on her until she didn't recognise the monster he had become. Why was he doing this? What had changed? This wasn't Neil – this wasn't her husband. Neil wasn't a bad man; he wasn't a brute.

It had been a perfect calamity of events. The pregnancy test had made him suspicious, and he had lashed out at her. He had always been the jealous type and, because she was on the pill, it was only natural that he would suspect she had been unfaithful if she was doing a test. Her stupidity had provoked him and resulted in the mess they were now in. But the very worst part wasn't the horrible names he had called her, the bruising, the swollen jaw or even the betrayal – it was that Anabel had witnessed it all. The poor child had been traumatised by what had happened and hadn't wanted to sleep alone in her own bed. Lucy had had to promise Anabel that he wasn't in the house before she would finally close her eyes and go to sleep, but Neil wouldn't stay away forever. What would happen when he did come home? Would Anabel be scared of her own father forever more? Lucy hated to think of the damage this might have done to her daughter at such a tender age.

Lucy was doing her best to raise Anabel properly;

she did everything it said in the parenting books and followed the advice she read online. When Anabel was a baby, Lucy had steamed organic fruit and veg for her to eat. She read her a story every night even when she was tired and longed to skip it. But, no matter how much work Lucy tried to put into being a good parent to Anabel, one punch from Neil had gone and unravelled it all. Would this be Anabel's overarching memory of her childhood? A blot on the copybook of her formative years. At five years old she was old enough to remember what had happened behind the walls of her home this evening. Her father had done this – the man she idolised had caused it all. Like a child peeping behind the curtain at a magic show, the illusion of her daddy was now shattered. Anabel had been so frightened that she had run next door – Lucy realised with sudden clarity that Anabel had thought that their strange neighbour Eileen was a safer option than her own father. That said it all really.

In fairness to their neighbour, she wasn't as odd as Lucy had originally thought. She had been quite nice actually and Lucy was very grateful to her. She had taken charge of the situation, giving her a warm cup of tea to sip as she tended to her swollen eye. And once the little dog had finally stopped barking, she had been a great distraction for Anabel in her shock. Maybe they had been too quick to judge her; they had made assumptions about Eileen and her life but what did they really know about her? She had been kind and compassionate in a crisis and, for that, Lucy would be forever grateful. There had been something about Eileen, a sadness or deep empathy in her eyes that Lucy could identify with.

After Eileen had gone home, Lucy had taken a deep breath and gone back into the bathroom. Her head throbbed and her ribs were tender to the touch. As she looked around the room, there was no sign of what had taken place just a short time earlier. She realised that Eileen must have cleaned the place up. She tugged on the cord to turn on the light above the mirror. She got a fright when she saw her reflection: the woman staring back at her was unrecognisable even to her – her face was grotesque. Her eye was puffy and closed and there was a gash above it which had thankfully stopped bleeding. She turned the light off and headed back into the bedroom where Anabel was sleeping in her bed. She looked down at her daughter, lost to the land of dreams, and stroked her smooth skin. What was she meant to say to Anabel in the morning to explain it? When Anabel had woken up and found her on the kitchen floor the last time, she had been confused and they had been able to fob her off, but now there would be no uncertainty in her young mind – she knew the terrible violence her father was capable of.

The last thing Lucy wanted was for Anabel to grow up and think it was okay for a man to hit her. She imagined Anabel thirty years from now, coming and telling her that her husband had hit her; without a shadow of a doubt, Lucy would order her to leave him – she wouldn't listen to excuses or explanations. She had read the books, she'd seen the posters in her GP's waiting room, she had heard the advice on TV chat shows. She would hear a woman on the radio telling her story and she would think *Why don't you just leave him?* or *He won't change.* She had never imagined that *she* would be the one in this situation, that the man she loved and that said he loved her would be capable of doing this to her. She had always thought it was black and white but now she realised that it wasn't so clear-cut. There were lots of murky grey shades in there too. And now their neighbour knew all about Neil's temper. Lucy had tried hard to convince Eileen that Anabel had been confused and that Neil hadn't done this to her, but she knew Eileen had seen right through her. The woman was a recluse, so she probably didn't have anyone to share the gossip with, but all the same, Lucy hated that someone else knew their business. Like smoke creeping under a door, their grubby little secret had escaped from beyond the four walls of their home.

15

It was after midnight when Lucy finally heard Neil's key in the front door downstairs. Dread and fear spilled into the pit of her stomach as his feet trudged up the stairs. What kind of mood would he be in? Would he still be angry? Or would he have calmed down by now? She sat up in the bed and flicked on the lamp on her bedside table. She grabbed her phone and held it in her hand, ready to call the emergency services if she had to. She didn't dare breathe as she heard him make his way down the landing and then the bedroom door opened. His outline appeared in the door frame but there was no anger in his eyes and instead they were filled with tears and such obvious contrition that her heart twisted. He looked smaller somehow, like a child who had got in trouble and was waiting for the punishment to be doled out. She put down the phone and hugged her knees in tight against her chest.

He glanced at Anabel asleep next to her. Her mouth was half-open in a gentle O, her small chest rising and falling in even beats. Water filled his eyes as he looked at their daughter.

'I'm so sorry,' he said, taking a step forward and crumpling onto the bed beside them.

And even though this was all his own doing, she hated seeing him in this state. His shoulders heaved with sobs and for ages no sound came out. It was like when Anabel fell and hurt herself and those seconds between the fall and the cry were excruciating.

'I-I don't know what came over me. It's like this rage descended on me and I wasn't myself any more. I never meant to hurt you... It was seeing that pregnancy test – I don't know – I just snapped... I'm not trying to make excuses, but I found out today that there's a new gym opening up around the corner and I'm stressed out of my bin that they're going to rob all my customers and close me down. How will we afford the mortgage on this place if the gym goes under? I'm under so much pressure trying to keep it all afloat. Then when you mentioned that you had thought you might be pregnant, I just lost it...' His voice sounded desperate; tinny and far away. 'But honestly, Lu, I'm so sorry.'

She nodded dumbly in agreement. This was awful for both of them; as much as she was angry with him, she hated seeing him in this grovelling mess. 'I'm sorry too.' And she was. She really was. Why hadn't she thought about it from his position? She had a role to play in all of this because maybe if she hadn't provoked him by bringing up the subject of having a second child and then going out and buying the pregnancy test, he wouldn't have snapped, and they wouldn't be in this mess right now. She wished there was an undo button, and they could go back to being the happy family that they had been before, but something told her deep down that they never would be. They would never be the same again. This was to be a defining moment in all their lives. But despite what he had done, she hated to see him this distraught. She ached seeing the man she loved in such turmoil. How could this be the same man who had beat her black and blue just hours earlier? How could she be scared of him? He was nothing more than a frightened little boy.

'Shh,' she soothed and pulled his head against her chest. He clung to her as he cried, and she felt pity well up inside her for him. He didn't want to be in this situation any more than she did.

'I'm a monster,' he cried. 'I don't deserve you.'

'It's okay,' she said, even though it wasn't okay – it would never be okay.

'It's not okay, look at what I've done to you!' he berated himself. 'Your beautiful face...' He reached out to stroke her forehead but she flinched from his touch.

'It's sore,' she explained.

'The test – well... was it positive?' he ventured.

She shook her head, feeling another rush of disappointment as she thought about how hopeful she had been just a few hours earlier. 'My period was late; I guess I got carried away by the idea.'

He nodded and she was sure she could see a wash of relief in his eyes. 'It's for the best,' he said.

She nodded.

'How is she?' he asked, looking forlornly at their daughter who was still sleeping soundly on the bed beside them.

'She's very upset, Neil. She ran next door and got the woman to help.'

His eyes widened and he visibly winced. 'She fetched Mad Mary from next door?'

Lucy bristled. 'Please don't call her that.'

'What?' He looked shocked; they always called her that, it was one of their little jokes.

'Her name is Eileen.' Lucy didn't know why, but she suddenly felt defensive of the woman.

He slumped down onto the bed. 'Annie must have been terrified. She was more afraid of me than the crazy lady next door – that says it all.' He shook his head in disgust.

'I told Anabel that it was an accident, that I fell over, but she's not stupid. She was really upset by it all. You'll have some bridges to mend with her.'

He hung his head and they both fell quiet, each locked inside their own thoughts. 'I'm turning into him...' he whispered after a moment.

She pulled away and looked up at him 'Who?' she asked.

'My dad.'

Neil never spoke about his dad. It was a no-go area. Lucy had tried to get him to open up over the years, but he would never talk about it. He would shut down all attempts so eventually she just avoided the subject, guessing that it was too painful for him. All Lucy knew was that he had left Neil's mother when he was seven and she had raised him on her own. His father had never made contact with them again. 'Did your dad hit your mum?' she ventured.

He nodded, his pupils wide with terror. 'I grew up hating him. I hated what he did to Mum, it terrified me. I swore I wouldn't be the same as him.' He gritted his teeth. 'I don't want to be like him,' he repeated again, with such vehemence in his voice that it chilled her. She had never seen him this worked up before.

'Neil, you're not him,' she soothed. 'It's okay, it's all going to be okay.' She felt a gnawing sense of doubt invade her; was it all going to be okay? Could they fix this or, well, she didn't want to think of the alternative...

'I'm so sorry, Lu. You have to believe me: that will never happen again. You know I love you; I'd never want to hurt you. I hate myself for what I've done.' His words were ringing in her ears. 'I don't want to be this person. I'm sorry, I promise you... I'll get help, whatever it takes, I'll do it.'

She knew he had learnt his lesson, and seeing how remorseful he was was almost more painful than the physical wounds he had inflicted upon her. 'It's okay, I know this isn't who you are.' He held his head in his hands as she rubbed his back in rhythmic circles.

'First thing tomorrow I'm going to get an appointment with a counsellor.'

She nodded. 'I think that's a good idea. You need to get help.'

He sucked in sharply and the air whistled between his teeth. 'I don't want to be like him,' he repeated.

'You're not your father, Neil. You've already taken the first step by admitting that you need help. We'll do this together and I'll be right by your side every step of the way.'

He pulled her into an embrace. 'I love you so much,' he sobbed into her hair. 'I don't deserve you.'

16

It was well into the small hours of the morning when I finally fell asleep. After listening out for next door and, reassuringly, hearing no sounds of drama after Neil arrived home, I eventually decided to call it a night and headed upstairs to bed. How could Lucy just let him waltz back into the house again like he had done nothing wrong? I wondered as I climbed under the duvet. Dora hopped up, circled several times before curling up near my feet like she always did. It was hard to fathom why Lucy didn't just throw Neil out after what he had done to her. But I guess sometimes we tell ourselves all kinds of lies in the blind optimism that things will get better. I of all people knew that.

I didn't hear my alarm go off the next morning and only woke when Dora started barking. I bolted upright in the bed. It took me a minute to get my bearings. Then I heard the doorbell. As the events of last night came rushing back to me, I whipped back the duvet and planted my two feet on the floor. I grabbed my fleecy dressing gown from the hook at the back of my bedroom door and myself and Dora raced downstairs. All kinds of thoughts flitted through my mind. Was little Anabel going to be standing there looking for my help once more? What if Neil had started up again? I knew I shouldn't have left them alone; I should have insisted that they come next door to stay the night with me. Why hadn't I called the Gardaí? Even if Lucy wasn't willing to admit what had happened at the hands of her own husband, maybe I should have reported it anyway, and at least that way there would be a record on file about it all.

I didn't even stop to check through the spyglass like I usually would; instead, I slid the chain up from its holder and twisted the latch. But it wasn't Anabel or Lucy, it was Tim, my key worker, standing there. He was wearing his big black puffa coat and chunky winter boots. His dark wavy hair was a little on the long side and it was falling over his eyes. I had completely forgotten about his visit today.

'Sorry, Eileen.' He smiled apologetically. 'I hope I didn't catch you at a bad time?' His eyes darted to my dressing gown before quickly looking away again.

'No, no, Tim, not at all,' I said, cursing myself for not remembering. I was mortified that he had caught me in my nightclothes. I checked my watch and saw it was just after 10 a.m. I never slept in late. I was always up and dressed when Tim called. He would be concerned about me now that I had broken the routine. He would probably make a note in my file and keep a closer eye on me. 'I had a bit of a late night last night,' I offered by way of explanation.

'Oh yeah?' he asked, clearly intrigued.

'I was over in a neighbour's house,' I said. Let him think I had a wild social life.

His eyes lit up like I knew they would. 'That's great that you've met the neighbours,' he effused. 'I know that was something that Savannah had mentioned on her last visit, so that's fantastic that you've made so much progress in that short space of time.' He beamed at me. He was delighted, God love him. That was the thing with Tim, he genuinely cared so much and wanted to see his patients moving on. I didn't have the heart to break it to him about the real reason why I was next door; let him think that I was sipping wine and nibbling canapés or whatever it was that people did in their neighbours' houses these days.

'Right, you go sit down in the living room and I'll go get dressed,' I said.

I hurried back up the stairs and into my bedroom. I noticed Dora hadn't followed me; the traitor had stayed downstairs with Tim. I opened my wardrobe. Three jumpers, a cardigan, a couple of T-shirts, two pairs of trousers, a pair of jeans and my coat were the only things hanging there. I lifted out the black trousers and put on a T-shirt, followed by my bobbly grey cardigan over it. I brushed my teeth, then ran a hairbrush through my hair. The grey was starting to take over, I thought, as I looked at my reflection staring back in the mirror.

I returned downstairs to Tim and found him sitting on the sofa with Dora lying beside him. He was tickling her behind her ears and then she rolled over onto her back and he scratched her belly. Tim always made a big fuss of Dora; I liked that about him. Dora was my barometer for people; if Dora didn't like you, then neither did I.

'Would you like a cup of tea?' I offered even though I knew he'd decline. He always did.

'No thanks, I'm fine, Eileen.' He was always so polite, and I guessed he didn't want to put me to the trouble.

'You may as well, I'm having one myself,' I said.

'Well, go on then, why not?' he said.

'Do you take milk? Sugar?'

'Just a drop of milk, please.'

I went into the kitchen and flicked the switch on the kettle. Thankfully, the two mugs that I owned were already washed and put back in the press. I plonked a teabag in both and waited while the water boiled. When the tea was made, I brought both mugs out and handed one to Tim.

'Thanks, Eileen.' He placed it on the coffee table and picked up his backpack. 'Now then,' he said, un-zipping it and taking out my file. 'I'm sorry I didn't make it the last time. I got married, so I had a few weeks off. Savannah said you were doing well though.'

'You're married?' I was shocked.

'We all have to settle down eventually.' He grinned sheepishly, but I could see the happiness in his eyes.

'Well, congratulations; married life clearly suits you.'

He was grinning like a little boy, clearly delighted with himself. Who was the lucky woman, I wondered. It was the first time he had ever told me anything about his private life. I realised that he knew every-thing about me, every painful detail, but I knew nothing about him. What did he like to do on the weekends? Was he outdoorsy as his clothes sug-gested? I imagined him and his new wife going for rambling forest walks together on their weekends. I could picture them cosying up in the evening after a long day in work, him chatting about his patients and her chatting about whatever it was that she did. She was probably a teacher or a nurse or some other kind of caring profession just like he was.

'So, how've you been doing, Eileen?' he asked, changing the subject away from himself.

'Very well, thank you.'

'You're looking great, you're obviously eating well and getting out in the fresh air.' I knew it was his way of asking if I was taking care of myself.

'I am,' I replied.

'Good, good, and everything is okay here with the house. No issues there?'

'All is good.'

'At this rate you won't need us any more.' He laughed, flipping the page in his notepad and scrib-bling something down. 'Did you think any more about the computer course I mentioned the last time I saw you? I think you'd be well able for it and as I said before, you could take it at your own pace. It would only be a few hours a week so it wouldn't be a huge time commitment and the skills would be useful in your daily life. Nearly everything is done on computers or through email nowadays.'

I shook my head. Here he was banging on again about the internet and technology, but I had no interest in any of that stuff. I didn't have a mobile phone, even though Tim was always pushing me to get one. I had a landline all right, but Tim was the only one who ever called me on it. He would laugh and say he didn't know how I survived without a mobile, but it baffled me that he actually thought I'd use one. Who would I be calling? 'I don't need any of that stuff,' I said firmly.

'All right, well sure keep it in mind anyway. Another thing I wanted to mention,' he continued, 'is if you would be interested in getting work in one of the local businesses? It wouldn't have to be anything too stressful. We have placed other clients in a warehouse in Drimnagh; now, it's nothing too taxing, mainly picking and packing orders. You'd be well able for it. Or else we could look at the supermarket and I know that the coffee shop in the village is crying out for staff at the moment. You could start off with a few hours until you got used to it and gradually build it up from there. It would be a few bob for you and would be a good way of getting out and meeting people. What do you think?' He pushed his hair out of his eyes and smiled kindly at me.

This was the problem with Tim, he was always pushing me on. He could never just let me be. Why wasn't the progress I had already made enough for him? I knew that he was only doing his job, but I had come so far from the woman who had moved in here last February, trembling in fear and full of doubts. I had never lived alone; as a child I had lived with my parents, then in my twenties when I got the job in the bank, I had lived in a flat with my friends. Not long after that I had met Dan and we had bought our own house and had a family. Then I had spent a long time in St Jude's. Although I had often lamented the lack of privacy or quiet time in that place, I'd never forget the silence on my first night alone in St Brigid's Road. It was deafening compared to the noise of St Jude's. Trolleys rattling, people shouting, people crying; that was my usual backdrop and I had grown used to it. In fact, it was comforting in its own way. On my first night in this house, I had lain there fully clothed on top of the bed because I wasn't sure if I'd stay the night or ask to be brought back to St Jude's. I hadn't thought I'd even last a night on my own.

I thought about my little room there, with the window overlooking the tarmacadamed car park, the narrow, steel-framed bed and small locker with the few possessions I had left: the clothes I had come in with and a gold link bracelet with a single feather charm that I had been given one year for my birthday. That place had been my whole world for almost ten years – I had never thought I would leave it. It had been a massive step, coming back out into the community and moving into this house on St Brigid's Road. No one was more surprised than me by how I had adapted and found my own routine.

'You've done so well over the last year,' he continued, trying to convince me. 'I was talking to the team about you at our case meeting yesterday, and we're all amazed at your progress and how you've coped with the independence. And wait until I tell them you've been in socialising with the neighbours!' He winked jokily at her. 'I know it might seem daunting to you, but we really think you're ready to take the next step now.' Dora licked his hand. The turncoat.

'And who would mind Dora?' I retorted. Did he really think I could just swan off to work all day and let the little dog fend for herself? I had responsibilities. Dora needed me.

He must have seen the doubt in my eyes because

he added, 'Have a think about it anyway... As I said, there's no pressure; we'll go at whatever pace you're comfortable with, but we want to support you and help you continue moving forward in the right direction.'

I looked down at my wrist and ran my fingers over the links of the bracelet. If I closed my eyes, I could still smell the candle wax from the melting birthday candles, the sulphur from the match as it was struck off the side of the box, the smiling faces and voices singing 'Happy Birthday' to me. Standing there looking at all the people I loved most gathered around me and yet tears were running down my face – not tears of happiness but worthlessness and guilt because I didn't deserve any of them. As my fingers clasped the cool metal of the bracelet, the pain still felt as raw now as it had back then. It was all I had left from that life now. That bracelet represented everything and nothing.

17

When Lucy woke the next morning, a headache thumped inside her skull. She guessed it was a combination of the bang from the night before and dehydration from all the tears she had cried. The bed beside her was empty; Neil had already left for work. He had clients booked in for their personal training sessions and despite everything that had happened, she knew he couldn't let them down. It was probably better that he was gone to work; what good would it do if the two of them sat at home moping and apologising and feeling awful about it all?

She pulled back the duvet, went into the en suite and tugged the cord on the light above the sink. Her face was still puffy, and her left eye was so swollen that she could barely see out of it. Overnight, the bruising on her face had grown darker and tawny-red blood was crusted along her brow. How could she possibly see anyone in this state? What would Anabel think? She found a facecloth and tried to clean off the sticky blood, but her skin was tender and sore as she dabbed it. She reached for her make-up bag and applied some concealer in an attempt to hide the worst of the bruising before Anabel got up, but despite her best efforts, the blue-black shade still shone through.

She left Anabel to sleep on as she went down to the kitchen and filled the water tank in her Nespresso machine. Neil had carried Annie into her own room and after staying up late into the night talking, they had eventually fallen into an exhausted sleep beside one another. It was the first time that Neil had ever opened up to her about his father and just how violent he had been. Lucy had had tears in her eyes as she lay there beside him, while he recalled the horrors he had witnessed growing up. Neil had been in a right state as he'd talked about the way his mother had been treated, the vicious beatings she had endured and how he had tried to intervene to help her. He would attempt to pull his father off her – literally clawing the man's fingers away from her neck – but he would just turn on Neil then. She imagined a six-year-old Neil trying to wrestle him off his mother, not realising that he hadn't a hope against a fully grown man, and then cowering in terror as the monster attacked him next. Lucy could see it physically pained him to relive those dark days again. It seemed he had suppressed all those brutal memories for a long time but last night the lid had been opened, and it had all come spilling out. It frightened Neil, that despite knowing the pain his father had inflicted on his mother, history was starting to repeat itself and he was doing the same thing now to his wife.

She had lain in the crook of his arm with her stinging face pressed against his chest, her mind spinning over everything that had happened. Despite everything, she felt closer to him now. She had seen him in his rawest form, she had witnessed him at his most vulnerable and she felt she understood him more. He wasn't a bad person; he had never worked through his childhood trauma, but he knew now that the time had come for him to face his demons and he had promised her that he would contact a counsellor first thing that morning and get started on the path to managing his anger. When they had got married, they had taken their vows for better and for worse. She had never imagined then that the vows they had made would be tested like this, but she would be by his side while he got the help he needed.

While the coffee spurted out of the machine and filled the mug, Lucy called Jenna and said she had a cold and that they would need to cancel their clients for that morning. She and Jenna were supposed to be doing a trial for a wedding party. Although it was only a test run, and could easily be rescheduled, she felt awful about letting the wedding party down. She hoped they would understand. She hated cancelling on people but what else could she do? There was no way she could get away with another excuse to explain the state of her face to Jenna. Jenna would see right through her. Her friend told her that she was doing the right thing by not coming into work and risking spreading her dose. She also couldn't face the looks she knew her battered face would attract from the parents at the school either, so she had given Anabel a day off too.

When Anabel got up, Lucy felt a smack of guilt as she noticed her daughter's eyes were bloodshot, from the combination of the late night and all the tears she had cried.

'Would you like pancakes for breakfast, Annie?' she offered. *Guilt food*, Lucy thought. *You're trying to sweeten your own child.*

Anabel scrunched her nose up in confusion. Pancakes were normally a weekend treat. 'But I have to go to school.'

'I thought we'd give it a miss today and have a duvet day instead, what do you think?'

Anabel's face lit up. 'Can we watch *Frozen*?'

'Again?' Lucy laughed. 'Are you not sick of that movie by now?' Even though Anabel had seen it a thousand times already and knew the whole film word for word, she still loved it, and her eyes would light up as Elsa twirled around her ice palace singing 'Let It Go'.

'No way.' She shook her head emphatically.

'All right then,' Lucy agreed.

She watched Anabel as she took small bites of the pancake; the child didn't mention the events of the night before and Lucy didn't bring it up either. *She must have questions*, Lucy thought as she watched her chew. She hadn't even remarked on Lucy's battered face which Lucy knew must be upsetting for Anabel to see. Lucy didn't know what to do – should she bring it up again this morning? She didn't want Anabel feeling scared or internalising her worries but, on the other hand, she didn't want to upset the child any more by reliving it all again. What was the right way to handle it? It wasn't as if she could ask someone: *'So you know when your child witnesses their father beating you up, how do you talk to them about it afterwards?'*

After breakfast, as Lucy sat on the sofa stroking her daughter's forehead, while Anabel sucked her thumb engrossed in the screen, she looked out the window and saw Eileen emerging from number 26. She was wearing a drab black coat and her short hair was tucked beneath a woollen hat that was pulled down over her ears. She had Dora's lead in one hand and her Tesco bag for life in the other. Usually, Lucy was at work during the day, so she never saw Eileen going anywhere. She briefly wondered if she should drop something in to her like a bottle of wine or a box of chocolates to say thanks. It would be awkward for the two of them, but she was grateful to Eileen for coming to her aid like that. She decided she would pick up something next time she was in the shop and drop it over.

* * *

Neil was sheepish when he came home from work that evening. His brows were knitted together, and his eyes were heavy with remorse when he saw her bruised face – and that was after all the layers of concealer. He walked straight over and hugged her close and she knew he was full of self-reproach. Anabel looked warily at him from her play area, but she remained where she was and didn't rush over to him like she usually would whenever he came in the door after work.

He handed Lucy an extravagant bunch of white roses.

'Hi, Anabel,' he called, but she ignored him and continued playing.

'How was your day?' he asked, turning back to Lucy as she untied the string that secured the flowers and placed them in a vase on the centre of the island. He had called her earlier to see how she was. He knew that she hadn't been able to go to work and had kept Anabel home from school too.

'I've had better,' she replied.

His gaze dropped to the floor. 'I have my first counselling session next week. It was the earliest appointment I could get.'

She nodded. 'That's good. I'm glad you're taking the first step.'

'Yeah, hopefully she can get me to work through this anger. I don't know why it's coming to the surface now...' He exhaled heavily. 'I thought I had left all that behind me...'

'These things often run far deeper than we realise.'

'Yeah, but I saw what my dad did to my mum, and I hated him for it. Why am I doing the same thing now to you?' He shook his head in despair. 'I can't understand it!'

'Talking to a professional will help you to get to the bottom of it all.'

He bit down on his lip. 'You and Annie – you're my whole world. I'm so sorry, I really am.' He shook his head. He looked so scared and vulnerable, and she just wanted her big, strong husband back, not this childlike little boy who seemed to have replaced him.

'I know this isn't you; you're going to get the help you need to overcome this and we'll get past it.'

'I'll never forgive myself.' Tears filled his eyes, and she knew that he meant it. She knew that he had been scared of the monster he had become, and the loss of self-control had been as frightening for him as it had been for her on the receiving end. Even if she forgave him – he would never absolve himself.

'Shhh,' she soothed, pulling him into a hug as she felt his warm tears against her neck. 'It's all going to be okay.' She wished he would forget about it; she just wanted to move on and block it out of her head.

18

The swelling subsided, the bruising faded, the wound knitted itself together and Lucy's eye opened up again, but the grief, the distrust, the way everything had changed between them because Neil couldn't take back his actions, had left a deeper scar. No matter how many times he said sorry, it couldn't undo what had happened. Remorse hung like a heavy chain around his neck, but Lucy just wanted him to stop grovelling and forget it had ever happened. Every time he brought it up or fussed over her or apologised, it took her back there again and she wanted to put it behind them.

In the end, Lucy had taken a full week off work.

She knew she couldn't go back until the bruising had faded. Jenna had held the fort and roped in a trainee make-up artist to cover for her to ensure they didn't let any brides down. Lucy didn't think she'd ever be able to repay her friend. She didn't send Anabel to school either. Lucy didn't like to think that they were hiding out in the house, but it certainly felt like they were waiting until she was ready to go back out and face the world again. The two of them stayed at home, watching movies, and snuggling up together on the sofa. Her mum had phoned her for a chat the day before and was surprised when Lucy said she wasn't at work. Lucy had told her she had taken the day off because she wasn't feeling well, and her mum had immediately offered to come over and take Anabel off her hands for a few hours and let her rest. Lucy had had to think quickly and said Anabel had come down with the bug too and they didn't want to pass it on. She hated lying to her mum but what could she do? She would be immediately suspicious if she saw the state of Lucy's face right now. Lucy had it under control and she didn't want to worry her mother.

As the days went on, gradually her face began to resemble itself a little more and the make-up started to conceal the dirty yellow pallor around her eye. It was obvious that Anabel was nervous around Neil; he had broken her trust, but Lucy noticed yesterday that she sat up on his knee when he came home from work, which felt like a major step forward. She was slowly beginning to warm to him again, but it was going to take time before he was back in her good books.

She had spotted Eileen several more times as she went to the shop with her little dog or with her hood up while she waited in the rain, following Dora around on the lead as she sniffed out a spot to go to the toilet. She hadn't gone next door to thank her yet and she knew, if she was being really honest with herself, the more the days went on, the less likely it was going to happen. She told herself it was because she hadn't been to the shop yet to pick up a box of chocolates, but really, she just couldn't face it. She wanted to pretend that the sorry incident had never happened and if she called next door, she would have to relive the whole thing all over again. And besides, Eileen probably wouldn't appreciate a visit from Lucy, any more than Lucy wanted to do it. She just wanted to forget about it and put that awful evening behind her and from the limited amount she knew of Eileen, she was pretty sure that she would feel the same way.

She glanced at the clock and saw it was just after five. Neil was probably sitting in the room with the counsellor at that very moment. She had been counting down the days until his first session. They both wanted to be doing something proactive to 'fix' this problem and start their path away from this nightmare. She wanted the old Neil back and this was the first step in that journey towards healing.

Eventually, she heard Neil's key in the lock, and she waited for him to appear in the kitchen.

'So, how did it go?' she asked as soon as he came through the door.

He stormed past her and slammed his keys down on the island. Lucy's heart sank. Clearly, it hadn't gone well.

'It was a complete waste of time.'

Thankfully, Anabel was upstairs having a bath. The last thing she wanted was for his erratic mood to unsettle their daughter and undo everything just as they were getting back on an even keel again.

'Why?' she asked.

'It's all bullshit.' He paced past her and opened the fridge.

'What happened?'

'She was asking me all these stupid questions.'

'About what?'

'She kept wanting to talk about my dad.' He shut the fridge without taking anything out.

'Well, it's kind of relevant,' Lucy said pointedly.

'I get that, but even after I told her about him, she kept digging for more. She just wouldn't let it go!'

'It's her job to get to know your past.'

'There's nothing more to know – he was a dick – he left us. End of story.'

'Come on, Neil,' she cajoled. 'She has to learn about your childhood.'

'She was asking me if I loved him? Did I feel torn in my love for my parents? How did I feel when he left?' He mimicked the therapist's voice. 'What kind of shit is that? My father was a prick, end of story. The best thing to ever happen to me and Mum was the day he left us. I have no feelings for that man.'

'But can't you see? She's trying to get to the root of why you lashed out like that. She has to unpick the past before you can piece it all back together again.'

'I want to forget about him and just fix the problem. I don't want to waste time thinking about him. I thought she'd be doing anger management techniques and useful stuff like that, not wasting time dwelling on all that old crap.' He exhaled heavily.

Lucy sighed. 'So, when is your next appointment?'

'I don't know.'

'Neil, come on, you promised me you would get the help that you need,' she pleaded.

'I am, Lucy – I went there today to get help, but she was shit.'

'Then you need to find a different counsellor. Maybe she's not the right one for you but there will be someone else who will be.'

'Look, I've learnt my lesson. I can put my hand on my heart and say it was the worst day of my life. I never want to feel like that again. I *know* I'll never do anything like that ever again. I'm ashamed of myself. I never want to go that low again.'

Lucy bristled and felt anger rise within. This wasn't what they had agreed. One appointment hardly constituted getting the help he needed to manage his temper. She was disappointed and angry. Like she was the only one taking it seriously.

'You promised me, Neil! You promised you would get the help you needed.' She felt the pressure of tears in her eyes. She had so much hope pinned on this appointment and now it felt like he had made no progress.

He moved closer to her and took her in his arms. 'No one regrets it more than me, I swear to you.

Seeing you upset – the state of your face.' He reached out and tenderly stroked her healing skin. 'Knowing Anabel is off with me and it's all because of what I did – that is enough for me to know that it won't happen again. I know I'll never lay another finger on you. I promise you. I swear on Anabel's life – I won't let myself do it.' He reached out and tucked her hair behind her ears. 'I promise you, Lu, it won't happen again.'

Lucy closed her eyes and breathed in deeply. She knew he regretted his actions and was paying the price now. She wanted to believe him. She so badly wanted everything to be okay between them again.

'I promise you,' he repeated, wrapping his arms around her, and she felt herself soften in his embrace. How was it that the same arms that gave her such comfort had been the ones that caused so much pain? 'It's never going to happen again.'

She opened her eyes and locked them with his. She stared into their grey-green depths.

'You have to promise me, Neil,' she said. 'Whatever about hurting me; I can't let Anabel see anything like that ever again. Ever. I love you, I love our family, I don't want to lose you, but it can never happen again. Do you understand? That was the last time,' she reiterated. 'No more chances.'

'I swear to you on Anabel's life, I'll never lay a finger on you again,' he whispered in her ear.

She felt his strong arms around her, pulling her tight against his chest. Could it be that simple? That he'd gone so low that he'd learnt his lesson and would never lose control again. She wanted it to be that easy.

19

From my usual spot at the side of the window I saw Neil was still going to work as usual every day; despite what he had done to Lucy, his routine hadn't changed. What worried me was that I hadn't seen Lucy's car leave the driveway in over a week. As far as I could see, Lucy hadn't set foot outside, and I hadn't seen Anabel going to school either or even play in the garden. I had purposely been keeping a close eye on their house from my window. I could hear the sounds of the TV coming from their living room and I saw the lights on, so I knew they were in there. I guessed Lucy didn't want anyone to see her battered face and she was hiding away until it had healed. Even though I knew she didn't want my help, I'd thought about calling next door to check on them, just to make sure that everything was okay, but I didn't want to interfere or to be seen as the nosy neighbour. Lucy hadn't been able to get rid of me quick enough the other night, but what she didn't realise was that I hadn't wanted to be there either. Somehow fate had thrown us into a situation that neither of us wanted any part in.

When I opened the fridge to make dinner, I realised that I hadn't purchased a chicken in the butcher's that week. I was still out of sorts after everything that had happened.

Dora and I always ate roast chicken on a Friday. It was our weekly treat to ourselves, and it helped that the leftovers could be used to make soups and dinners for the coming week. I had never given Dora dog food; I didn't think a dog like Dora would appreciate bland dog nuts, so she ate whatever I ate. One time when Tim had seen me shredding a piece of chicken into smaller pieces, adding some mashed potato and mixing it all together with a splash of gravy and then putting in Dora's bowl, he had said she was the luckiest dog alive but I had told him that it was me who was the lucky one, because out of all the doorsteps that Dora could have waited on, she had chosen mine.

My knees creaked as I bent down and scoured the cupboards. I was only fifty-four but some days I felt ancient. After opening the doors and searching each press, all I found was a box of Cup a Soups and a bag of porridge oats. I took out a measly sachet of powdered soup and held it up to Dora.

'What do you think, D?' I asked.

Dora cocked her head and whined at me.

'Ack, all right then,' I sighed, 'we'll go to the shop. Go get your lead.' The butcher's would be closed at this time, but we'd still be able to get a chicken in the supermarket.

Dora hurried over to the door where her lead hung from the handle. She jumped up and tried to paw the lead down. I put on her little winter jacket. Winter had arrived with her frosty nip. The weather had turned bitter and, as a short-haired breed, I didn't want her feeling the cold. Tim had given the jacket to me for my birthday a few months ago. When he had handed me the present, I had been confused at first.

'It's for your birthday,' he had prompted.

I hadn't even realised it was my birthday – those days had long ago lost significance for me. 'Oh, yeah, of course.' I had taken it from him and held it in my hands.

'Go on, open it,' he'd encouraged.

I had felt self-conscious opening the gift in front

of him, but I had slowly torn the wrapping paper to reveal a tiny blue and red tartan jacket.

'It's for Dora,' he had added by way of explanation. 'I saw it in the shop and thought it would look cute on her. I know technically it's not really a present for you, but I hope you like it.'

'A jacket for a dog?' I had tutted, trying to hide the emotion that was flooding through me. 'What is the world coming to!' I had rolled my eyes. I cringed now at the memory. Despite my scornful reaction, the truth was that I was touched by his kindness. He had remembered my birthday and then gone to the trouble of buying something for me. It had been a long time since I had got a birthday present. I would never admit it to Tim, but it was one of the most thoughtful gifts I had ever received. I had bent down then and tried it on Dora and Tim was right, she did look adorable with it on.

Then Tim had produced a small cake and, mortifyingly for me, he had even gone to the trouble of lighting a candle and getting me to blow it out. I had to stop him before he started singing 'Happy Birthday'.

'Have patience,' I chided as I tried to do the clip on Dora's jacket. The dog was yelping and spinning around in anticipation. 'I won't be able to get it on if you don't stand still.' When I eventually had Dora dressed, I slipped my arms into the sleeves of my own coat, pulled my woolly hat down over my ears and flipped up my hood over it. Then I clipped the lead to Dora's collar, and we set off together.

Early winter darkness had already fallen as we stepped outside. Chimneys puffed out smoke into the cool night air and the street was eerily quiet as if the damp air had blanketed down the sound. An easterly wind howled down St Brigid's Road, so I pulled my zip right up to the top and tucked in my chin to avoid the piercing wind. The street lights had soft focus under the damp mizzle. I looked next door to see if I could spot Lucy or Anabel, but they had already drawn their curtains. I continued on, passing the houses of my neighbours. Theo and Chris must still be at work; their house was cloaked in darkness. The bins were still outside number 21. They had been left out since bin day on Monday, so I guessed they were away. I wondered if they were somewhere sunny, somewhere warmer than here. The fuzzy glow of car lights fused with the misty air as the rush-hour traffic crawled along beside me.

When I reached the supermarket, I made my way over to the lamp post where I usually tied Dora but there was a gang of teenagers standing with their hoods pulled up hanging around outside the entrance. I hated leaving Dora tied up; it always made me anxious should anyone come and try to steal the little dog. It was one of the reasons I usually only went in the daytime. I bent down and tied the lead around the steel post. As I looked down at Dora, the little dog looked as nervous as I felt. What could I do? They had a strict no-dogs policy in the store. I had once tried to carry her inside in my arms, but the manager had asked me to leave the shop, said it was 'off-putting to the other customers' – whatever that meant.

'I'll only be a minute,' I said to Dora to reassure her, but I could see the worry in her deep brown eyes. Dora wasn't like other dogs, she felt things just like humans did, I was sure of it. I hurried into the shop and straight down to the refrigerated aisles and found the poultry fridge. I quickly made my way to the checkouts, but my heart dropped when I saw queues snaking from every till. I had forgotten how busy the supermarket would be at this time on a Friday evening. The self-scan tills were the same and I hated those things anyway – they made me nervous, and I'd inevitably press the wrong button and get stuck waiting on one of the staff to come help me and it would take twice as long as it should. I stood in line as trolley loads were unloaded onto the conveyor belt in front of me. The longer I waited, the more the panic worked its way up inside me. Poor Dora would be getting stressed; what if the teens did something to her?

The woman in the queue ahead of me turned around and flashed me a smile of solidarity. 'You wouldn't want to be in a hurry,' she said, rolling her eyes towards the queue. 'You've only got one thing; do you want to jump ahead of me?' she offered, nodding at the chicken I was clutching.

Normally, I didn't believe in skipping queues; everyone's time was important. You had to put up with what life dealt you and if that happened to be a long supermarket queue then so be it, but Dora was outside all alone and probably scared to death. I nodded gratefully to the woman and went to move past her when she said, 'Eileen Prendergast, is that you?'

Her eyes were wide with disbelief. It had been a long time since anyone had called me by my married name. It took me a moment, but I remembered her too. It was her tone of voice I recognised. She looked older now, of course, and she was a little heavier than I remembered. Her hair was dyed a deeper shade of brown and her face was lined and jowly around her mouth. Ruth McKeever. I had once been so jealous of this woman – how organised and together she had always been, making life look easy. Even though she had two children as well, she never seemed to be frazzled like me who found even the simplest of tasks overwhelming. In those days, I always felt like I was two steps behind everyone else, always trying to catch up. Like I was running to a place, but I wasn't sure of the destination, when everyone else seemed to know exactly where to go and what they were supposed to be doing.

The sounds in the supermarket seemed to get further away; the grumbling from the other customers in the queue got fainter, the incessant beep-beep-beep of the checkouts faded into the distance and suddenly I was right back there again with the baby screaming, red-faced with fury, his two tiny fists flailing about in the pram, me fumbling with the buckle and Ruth leaning over, trying to help me. Ruth had lifted him out, put him up onto her shoulder and he had calmed instantly. Miraculously, he had stopped crying. And even though I knew that Ruth was only trying to help, how inept and ashamed I had felt, that even that simple task had been too much for me. That Ruth was the one who had been able to pacify him. Weren't babies supposed to know their own mother's scent? Well, my baby clearly had no preference for me or anyone who picked him up. Ruth had been kind and said things like, 'We all have bad days' and 'Newborns are hard work'. She had told me how when her own daughter was a baby, she had knowingly let the dinner burn because the baby had finally fallen asleep on her, and she didn't want to risk waking her by getting up to turn off the cooker.

The story of perfect Ruth McKeever burning the dinner had stuck in my head and I had gone home feeling a little better about myself. But then Dan had arrived home from work and said that Ruth had phoned him at the office saying that she'd met me in the supermarket. He said that Ruth claimed she was worried about me. I had felt humiliated and betrayed that Ruth had called my husband and they had discussed me. *Poor Eileen,* I imagined Ruth saying in a faux-concerned tone. Dan had given out to me then and asked why couldn't I get it together? People were starting to notice, he said. They were starting to talk. Why was I so pitiful? Why couldn't I cope like every other mother did? He said he was trying to work full-time and he shouldn't have to be dealing with this too when he came home from work. I could see the contempt for me burning in his eyes, the frustration that I couldn't do what seemed to come so easily to every other woman. Our friends, our neighbours. *What was wrong with me?*

My hands felt clammy standing there in the queue. The chicken slipped from my grip, dropped to the floor and landed with a thud at my feet. I saw heads swivel to see what the commotion was. I ran towards the sliding doors at the entrance. I could hear Ruth calling after me, 'Eileen? Eileen, are you okay?' But I didn't stop or turn around, I kept going towards the door. By the time I reached Dora, I was trembling. The teenagers were all gathered around watching something on one of their phones and didn't seem to be paying any heed to the little dog.

'C'mon, old girl,' I said, my hands shaking, fumbling with the lead. After a few failed attempts, I eventually managed to untether Dora and the two of us hurried out of the car park together. What were the chances of bumping into Ruth again after all this time? Just as I was starting to move on with my life. What if Ruth followed me home? She could find out where I lived... She might tell Dan. *Would he even want to know*, a voice inside my head mocked. I realised with a sting that he probably wouldn't care where I was. If he had wanted to find me, he would have by now; it wouldn't be too hard.

Panicked thoughts were spinning around my head

as I hurried along the concrete pavement and I reached St Brigid's Road before I even realised. At my gate I checked behind me once more and saw there were no cars, and no one was following me. I took a deep breath and continued up the path to my front door. I noticed Mr Muscle's car in the driveway next door. I put my key in the lock and closed it behind me and put the chain across it too. Back inside the safety of my own home, my heart rate began to slow once again, as I finally started to relax. I was doing so well these days – Tim was always telling me that – but I knew it was as fragile as the wings of a butterfly. Seeing Ruth had made me feel so vulnerable and exposed. Dublin was a small place; I knew my past would catch up with me one day. These things always did. I had been waiting for my day of reckoning to come; I couldn't hide from it forever and something told me that this was the start of the unravelling.

20

Life went back to normal for Lucy. Neil hadn't returned to the counsellor after his disastrous first session and she didn't push it with him. He swore he had changed, and she desperately wanted to believe him. She had gone back to work the Monday after; she had missed nearly two weeks of work in the end. She was able to disguise the last of her bruising with make-up. Anabel had returned to school too and she had given the child a note explaining that she had been sick. Anabel still hadn't spoken about what had happened that night and Lucy hoped she had put it out of her head. When they reached the school gate, she had a moment of panic that Annie might let it slip to her teacher if she enquired why she had been out of school.

'Annie love, if your teacher asks you why you weren't in, just tell her you were sick, yeah?' she prompted.

Anabel had looked at her wide-eyed and serious. 'Mammy, I can't lie to teacher.'

She bent down to her daughter's level. 'It's only a white lie, pet. If we told her the truth that we were having duvet days and watching movies, I don't think she'd be very impressed,' Lucy explained.

'Okay, Mammy,' Anabel reluctantly agreed.

'Good girl.' She kissed her on the forehead. 'You'd better hurry up and join your line.'

She watched her daughter traverse the playground to where the other children had lined up in their class group. Anabel spotted her friends, ran straight over to them and was immediately enveloped inside the group. She was such a social child; she loved being around other children. It made Lucy think about the visit from her mother the day before. She had surprised her by calling over proffering a Pyrex dish wrapped in tinfoil.

'Mum!' Lucy had said in surprise when she saw her on the doorstep.

'It's just a lasagne,' Noleen had said, walking straight into the house. 'I thought you could probably use a dinner after the couple of weeks you've put in. That was some dose you had. How's Annie feeling?' Lucy felt a stab of guilt; her mum had been phoning her every day to see how they were doing and each time Lucy had lied and said she was still sick. She had had so many messages from the mums of Anabel's school friends checking in to see if Annie was okay and Lucy hated herself for lying to them about her child being ill.

'I think she's turned a corner today actually.'

Annie came running down the hall. 'Grandma!' she cried. She threw her arms around the older woman.

'Well, she seems fine to me,' she laughed. 'How are you feeling, sweetheart? Did you have a nasty bug?'

Anabel wrinkled her nose in confusion and Lucy silently prayed she wouldn't out her. 'Me and Mammy snuggled up on the couch and watched lots of movies.'

'Sometimes that's the best medicine,' Noleen said with a wink.

Lucy said a silent thank you as she led her mother

down to the kitchen and made a pot of tea while Anabel went over to play with her toys.

'Is it the light in here or is your face bruised?'
Noleen said, taking off her glasses and peering at Lucy
as she filled the kettle from the Quooker tap. Lucy was
thankful she had put on make-up that morning. Even
though she hadn't left the house, Lucy was still applying
make-up for her own sake more than anything. Every
time she looked in the mirror or caught a glimpse of her
reflection in the patio doors, it all came rushing back to
her and at least the make-up helped to conceal it a bit.

'Oh that,' she said, thinking on the spot. 'I let Anabel do face paint on me yesterday and it's not coming
off.'

Noleen laughed and shook her head. 'The things
us mums do for our kids.'

Lucy placed the pot of tea down on the table,
poured two mugs and passed one to her mum.

'So, where's Neil today?'

'He had to go into work for a couple of hours.'

'On a Sunday?'

'He can't get staff; one of his personal trainers quit
last week, didn't even work out his notice period, and
another is out sick.'

Noleen shook her head. 'Poor Neil; he must be

under a lot of pressure. It's the time of year for all these horrible bugs doing the rounds.' Noleen clasped the mug in her hands, leaned across the table and lowered her voice. 'So did you get the chance to talk to him about number two yet?'

Her mum had been asking her for a while now if they were going to give Anabel a brother or sister. Noleen had assumed they were having difficulties and had delicately raised the subject with Lucy a few months back, but when Lucy had eventually confessed that Neil didn't want another child, Noleen had been concerned. Now Lucy regretted ever telling her mother because whenever she saw her she brought it up again and, after all that had happened, Lucy just wanted to move on and forget about it. She was just starting to come to terms with the fact that Anabel would be an only child. Although they hadn't discussed it again, Lucy knew that Neil wasn't going to relent. She had come to the realisation that if she wanted her happy family back the way they were before everything had started to go wrong, then she needed to forget about having another baby. She was working hard on changing her mindset to appreciate everything she had, instead of what she didn't have. And now her mother's prying questions would unravel it all.

'Mum – I don't want to talk about it.' Tears filled her eyes.

'Oh, love, what is it?' Noleen was concerned.

Lucy took a moment to compose herself and push back the tears. 'I've decided that I'm happy with what I've got.'

'He's not budging then?'

Lucy shook her head. 'We can't afford it.'

'That's nonsense.' Noleen shook her head so her blonde bob swished from side to side. 'Sure, look at the fancy car Neil drives; does he really need an Audi under his arse? Couldn't he trade it down for something smaller?'

'It's not just that, we don't have the space,' Lucy explained, using the same excuses that Neil had so often given her. 'We've only two bedrooms.'

'Look, I know it's none of my business but don't let it go too long or you might regret it and it'll be too late then. Anabel is growing up fast; now is the right time before she gets any bigger. You don't want her to be an only child, do you?'

'I'm happy with what I've got, Mum,' she lied. 'Lots of families just have one child these days. And besides, Anabel is so easy now at this age. The thoughts of going back to sleepless nights and nappies...' She shuddered to give effect.

'It's only a short-term pain; they don't stay small for long, Lu. When your dad and I had you three, we hadn't a pot to piss in – excuse my language. Times were a lot harder back then. We couldn't afford a house of our own, so we were stuck renting, we had one car and only one income coming in. There were no holidays abroad, we were lucky if we got a caravan in Wexford for a week, but despite all that, they were the happiest days of my life when you were all small and getting under my feet.' She laughed. 'In my experience, these things have a way of working themselves out. I know money might be tight for a little while if you take maternity leave, but I could help you out for a bit. You'll never regret a little baby, Lucy. You and Neil both have good jobs and a nice lifestyle; you'll find a way to make it work if you really want to. Why don't you have a chat with him again? Tell him how you're feeling about it all,' Noleen suggested.

Lucy felt herself bristle. Didn't her mother realise that she had tried this already? She had tried so hard and look where it had got her. He had sent her flying across the kitchen! How could she ever begin to explain to her mother just how opposed to having a second baby Neil was? Lucy could spend years trying to convince him and she knew that he still wouldn't change his mind.

Lucy shook her head. 'I think it's time to accept that Anabel will be an only child, Mum.'

Noleen reached across the table and squeezed her daughter's hand. 'If that's what you truly want, Lu, I'm happy for you, but just make sure this is what you really want. I don't want you to have any regrets.'

21

I was shaken for days after bumping into Ruth McKeever. The last time I had seen her she lived in County Louth; what was she doing in Dublin? Had she moved here? Did she live nearby? If so, was I going to bump into her again? It played on my mind like a bad video reel and made me think about things I hadn't thought about in years. Things I had pushed down inside me were suddenly surfacing again and I didn't like it at all. All the old hurtful words and feelings. The confusion of that time; waking up looking at the pale green walls in the hospital wondering where I was and what was going on and then remembering all over again – my whole world crashing down around me, day after day after day. I often thought about where my family were now. What they were doing with their lives. Did they ever think of me? Did they even remember me? I hoped not; I hoped they had rid their minds of me and my reprehensible actions. I hoped they had forgotten all about me. I didn't deserve them. What kind of person would do what I did? It was like looking back at a different person entirely. I was unrecognisable even to myself but what scared me the most was that I knew the chasm between the old me and this me was as fine as gossamer and I was so afraid I'd slip back there again.

It took me a few days to build up the courage to go back to the supermarket. Dora and I survived on the dregs we found in the cupboard. I knew if I bumped into Ruth again, I wouldn't be able to run away like I had the last time – I'd probably caught her off guard that evening, but she'd be ready for me now and she wouldn't let me run away so easily. She would have to interfere – that was the kind of person she was. She had never been able to just mind her own business.

Dora had started to get angsty that I was cutting our walks short. Although I still brought her around St Brigid's Road, she always tugged on the lead, planting her feet stubbornly on the footpath at the junction where we would usually turn on to the road that led to the shops. So when we ran out of the essentials like milk and firelighters, I had no choice but to head out. I kept my hood up and my gaze down so I wouldn't make eye contact with anyone the whole way around the supermarket, and I was relieved when we got home without seeing anyone. I was making my way up the path when I saw Lucy's car turn into their driveway. I guessed she was coming home from work. Anabel was in the back seat. I was glad to see they were leaving the house again and normal routines seemed to have been restored. I had been worried about them as the days had passed by and they hadn't gone anywhere. I was keeping a close eye on them and listening out for any sounds of a disturbance, but thankfully it had all been quiet in number 28.

I took my time opening the door and waited for them to get out of the car.

'Hi, Eileen,' Anabel called across the wall to me. 'Mammy, can I pet Dora?' she begged. She was bundled up in a big puffa coat and cerise-pink furry earmuffs covered her ears, her blonde hair falling in wispy tendrils down her back.

'Only for a minute,' Lucy warned. 'I need to start dinner.'

Anabel ran over to my garden and bent down to Dora, leaving Lucy and I to make polite conversation with one another over the wall. Dora's stubby tail bounded from left to right as Anabel made a fuss of her.

'It's a cold one,' I said to make conversation.

'It is,' Lucy agreed, shivering. Silence fell between us, and I knew we were both thinking back to that night in the bathroom. The glamorous, well-put-together woman standing before me now looked nothing like the mess I had found lying on the floor that evening. Her face had healed nicely and there were no scars to tell anyone what had happened. It was hard to believe that it was the same person. Lucy always seemed so composed, so self-assured. Neither of us mentioned the incident that night and I was glad of it. Although these things were never usually isolated events, I prayed that Neil had learnt from his actions and would change his ways. People could change; I was living proof of that.

Lucy began shifting from foot to foot to keep warm. 'Right, Anabel, c'mon,' she said after a minute, 'it's too cold to be standing out here.'

'Bye, bye, Dora,' Anabel said, standing up. 'Bye, Eileen.' She lifted her tiny, gloved hand and waved at me before following her mother into the house.

When Tim called for his next visit, he knew that something was off with me. I wanted to tell him about meeting Ruth in the supermarket and how it had unsettled me, but something made me hold off. I guess I was afraid that he'd suggest making contact with them again. He had brought it up once before, said it would help me in my recovery. I knew if I told him now that I was thinking about my family, he'd tell me that maybe the time had come to try and make peace with them. He was always telling me that I had to forgive myself but how could I after what I did? I knew for as long as I lived, I never could. I had closed the book on that part of my life a long time ago and there was no going back there now. It wasn't fair to anyone.

Tim wrinkled his brow in concern and asked me if I was all right; he checked whether I was sleeping and eating okay. He asked if I felt that my medication needed to be reviewed. All the time making little notes in my file. I told him I was fine. He then asked me if I'd any plans for Christmas. I knew he was just making conversation, but really, what a ridiculous question! What plans would I have? I knew Christmas was coming and I couldn't avoid it. All the houses on the street had put up lights. Theo and Chris in number 30 had sophisticated white lights draped around the bare branches of the cherry blossom tree in their garden and the weekend before I had seen Mr Muscle from next door climbing up on a ladder to put up colourful strip lights that looked like something from an American movie. I had been tempted to go over and give the ladder a little push while he was up there.

This was the first Christmas where I would be spending it on my own. For the last few years, I had spent my Christmases in St Jude's and, although they had been sombre affairs, they had been surprisingly lovely days. A choir would sing for us in the morning, and we were always given a gift. We would have a rubbery turkey and overcooked vegetables for dinner. Children from the local primary school always donated tubs of sweets, tins of USA biscuits and Chocolate Kimberleys and we'd sit around in the evening in the TV room watching *It's a Wonderful Life* and passing around the treats. Some of the residents were lucky and had visitors but there were a few like me, 'the lifers' we called ourselves, that never saw anyone. We all had people we were thinking about though, people we didn't see any more for all sorts of reasons that we never spoke about. Sometimes during a quiet moment in the day, the pain would rise up like a wave in my chest and threaten to wash me away but, despite everything, I can only look back on those days with fondness.

I shook my head and shrugged at Tim. 'It's just another day.'

'Well, maybe your neighbours might invite you round for Christmas drinks,' he said cheerily. I had mentioned meeting my neighbours once, and now Tim thought I had a hectic social life, dropping in and out of all the houses on the street. 'And what about putting up a little tree?' he suggested.

I shook my head. 'And spend my time sweeping up pine needles? No thank you.'

'Well, you could always do a small artificial one,' he tried. 'There are loads of options these days.'

I shook my head and tutted. 'It'd only be myself and Dora looking at it; such a waste.'

I used to love Christmas once upon a time, but it was a time for families and, when you lived on your own, it lost its appeal.

'Rightio. And you're sure that you're okay?' he repeated, scribbling something in his notebook.

'I've never been better, Tim,' I replied.

'You know I'm off over Christmas and I won't be back until the first week in January. Savannah is covering me again while I'm away so I'll leave you her number in case you need anything between now and then.'

'Where are you off to?' I enquired.

'We're spending Christmas with my wife's parents in England.'

'Well for some!' My tone was sardonic, and he started to blush. He seemed embarrassed by my teasing.

'You can call this number if you need anything. It's a twenty-four-hour line.' He reached out and pressed a leaflet into my hand.

'I'm grand, Tim, honestly. You don't need to worry about me.' He stood at the door, almost reluctant to leave.

'Go on, get out of here. I've things to be doing. You go and enjoy your first Christmas with your new wife.'

'Happy Christmas, Eileen.'

'Happy Christmas, Tim.'

22

Lucy was counting down the days until Christmas. Work had been hectic; it had been back-to-back Christmas parties and winter weddings and she had been putting in long hours. Neil had been working hard too; he was trying to cover his staff shortages by staying late in the evenings and working weekends so they both badly needed the break.

Even though he hadn't returned to the counsellor like he had promised, Neil seemed to be a changed man. He was dealing with his stress better and wasn't wound up like a tightly coiled spring, as he had been for the last few months. She had also changed; she knew not to push his buttons and didn't mention having another baby and, for the most part, things had returned to the way they were before.

Christmas morning arrived and Anabel woke them just after 5 a.m. They threw on their dressing gowns and hurried downstairs to see what Santa had brought. Things were back to normal between Neil and Anabel; Neil had won back her trust and Anabel seemed to have forgotten about what she'd seen in the bathroom that night.

Lucy peered out the window and saw the only houses with lights on were ones with young children like them. All their neighbours had put up outdoor lights; everyone except for Eileen. She didn't even have a tree displayed in the front window like everyone else. Lucy wondered what Eileen had planned for the day. Had she any family or someone to spend the day with? She hoped she had. It seemed unthinkable to her that a person would spend Christmas Day alone in her house with just her dog for company.

Lucy had invited Theo and Chris and some of the other neighbours over for mulled wine and mince pies three nights ago. She had thought about inviting Eileen too, but then thought twice. It would be awkward for everyone, and she knew Neil wouldn't be happy. He couldn't stand the woman; her very presence next door infuriated him. Also, Lucy was conscious that Eileen knew more about her family than she was comfortable with. Eileen now knew their deepest, darkest secret and she would spend the whole evening feeling uncomfortable and thinking back over that night again if Eileen joined them. Anyway, Eileen probably would just decline her invitation anyway. She didn't seem to like people; she never seemed to mix or have people call over. She was such an odd woman; except for her daily walk with her terrier, she was borderline reclusive. Besides her dog, it looked as though she had no one. That dog was her whole world.

'Look, Annie, I wonder what's in this one?' Lucy said, lifting a box and giving it a shake. Anabel started to tear open the gift wrap on her presents but looked disappointed when she got to the last one.

'Is that all my presents?' she asked, looking around the room. 'Is there anything else for me?'

'Anabel,' Neil said crossly. 'Don't be so spoilt! Santa brought you a lot of toys; you should be more grateful.'

'But I wished for a new baby; I put it in my letter.'

'I don't remember seeing that in your letter?' Lucy said, feeling mildly panicked that Anabel was now claiming that she had wanted a doll. She was sure there had been no mention of one but maybe she had missed it somehow.

'I wrote another one and put it up the chimney for Santa. I told him he could leave all the other things off my list because I wanted a new baby the most.'

'Oh dear, the second letter must not have arrived.' Lucy let out a sigh of relief. 'Maybe we could get you a doll for your birthday?' she suggested.

'No, Mammy.' She shook her head vehemently. 'I don't want a doll; I want a *real* baby.'

'Oh, sweetie,' Lucy said, crushed. 'I already told you Santa can't bring babies.'

A few weeks before Christmas, Anabel had asked her if Santa could bring her a baby brother or sister because Sinéad in her class had got a new baby from Santa. Lucy didn't know what Sinéad's parents had told her, but she had carefully explained to Anabel that Santa couldn't bring babies.

'But Sinéad's mammy said that Santa brought their baby,' Anabel insisted.

'It must have been a doll,' Neil tried.

'No, it was a real baby, Daddy. He's Sinéad's brother; his name is Patrick.'

'I promise, sweetie, Santa didn't bring that baby. Babies come from a mammy's tummy; you know that.'

'No, Mammy, you're wrong. Sinéad's mammy told-ded her that he did!'

'Well, look, this is what Santa has brought you,' Neil said, growing tired of the conversation.

Anabel walked away looking deflated, but what could they do? They had to be honest with the child.

Neil looked at her darkly as Anabel left the room. 'What was that all about? Did you put her up to it?' he accused.

'Of course not.' Lucy was affronted. 'Do you really think I'd do that to the child? She's devastated. Christmas is ruined for her! I had no idea she was pinning all her hopes on getting a new brother or sister.'

'Well, where did she get the stupid idea from then?'

'I don't know.' Lucy sighed in frustration. 'Someone in her class said that Santa had brought them a new baby. I don't know if that's what the parents told their child or if Anabel picked it up wrong. I told her that Santa can't bring babies but she was adamant.'

Neil exhaled heavily. 'What kind of parents tell their kid that Santa brings babies? Bloody ridiculous,' he muttered as he stood up. 'I'd better get the turkey in the oven.'

They were having Neil's mum, Pamela, Lucy's parents and her two brothers, Kyle and Mark, for dinner. She knew her larger family tended to overshadow Neil's – it was just him and his mum – but they both wanted their families there for Christmas.

Lucy set to chopping vegetables and Neil stuffed the turkey before putting it in the oven.

When their guests arrived, Anabel showed them her new toys. As Lucy watched her daughter demonstrating to her uncle Mark how her toy camera worked, she noted with a sense of relief that she seemed to have got over her earlier disappointment.

While Neil looked after the dinner, Lucy opened a bottle of champagne and filled everyone's glasses.

'To family,' she toasted.

'To family,' they all chorused in return.

When the dinner was finally ready, they squashed in around the table to eat. Lucy had spread a green runner down its length and a candelabra with six tapered candles made the centrepiece. She had taken time to decorate it with sprigs of holly and eucalyptus and each place setting was marked with a pine cone.

'This looks delicious. Well done, Neil,' her father, Pete, said, eyeing up the bronzed turkey standing in the centre of the table alongside bowls of sprouts, honey-roasted carrots and crispy roast potatoes. He nodded across the table at Pamela. 'You raised him well.'

'Ah, he was a good boy; he made it very easy on me.' She smiled adoringly at her son. Despite her self-deprecation, her face shone with pride as she looked at Neil. Recently, Lucy had been looking at Pamela in a new light as she thought about the beatings that Neil had described so vividly. It was hard to imagine that the same confident woman seated across the table from her had once been a victim at the hands of her own husband, but Lucy realised with searing irony that people would say the same about her if they knew the truth. She quickly pushed the thought from her head. What Neil had done to her was different. His father had been a monster by all accounts; Neil wasn't like that.

'Doesn't your neighbour celebrate Christmas?' Lucy's brother Kyle was asking, dragging her out of her thoughts. 'It's the only house on the street without any lights up.'

Lucy shook her head. 'We don't really know much about her, to be honest. She lives alone.'

'No, she doesn't,' Anabel interrupted. 'She lives with her dog called Dora.'

'Well, we can't forget Dora,' Lucy laughed. 'Annie is obsessed with her.'

'Poor woman. I hate to think of anyone being alone on Christmas Day,' Pamela remarked as she cut up her turkey.

'She's crazy,' Neil said, lifting some sprouts onto his plate. 'She probably doesn't even realise it's Christmas.'

'No, she's not, Daddy, she's very nice,' Anabel said.

'There's you told,' Pamela said, raising her eyebrows theatrically at the other grown-ups around the table.

'Did you like your presents from Santa, Anabel?' Pete asked.

Anabel nodded enthusiastically. 'He forgotted one thing though.'

Oh no, thought Lucy, *here we go...*

'What was it?' Pete continued.

'I wanted a new baby brother or sister and he didn't bring me it.'

The adults exchanged looks with one another around the table.

'Oh dear,' Pamela laughed. 'Santa doesn't bring babies, Anabel.'

'The sleigh would be too cold for them,' Pete said. 'They'd perish.'

'But he branged Sinéad one!' Anabel said.

'It's *brought* – he brought Sinéad one,' Neil corrected.

Lucy could see that Anabel was getting worked up again and she wanted to change the subject. 'Annie, sweetheart, we've been over this, remember?'

'I think someone is trying to tell you that it's time for number two,' Noleen said, winking at Pamela.

'Yes, you two, I've been wondering what the delay is,' Pamela chimed in, raising her wine glass to her lips and taking a generous sip. 'Get a move on.' She elbowed Noleen beside her and the two women threw their heads back in laughter.

'Well, maybe the stork hasn't been round this way recently,' Pete said, trying to be diplomatic.

'Oh, I think the stork knows very well where this house is,' Noleen retorted and looked pointedly across the table at Neil.

Although Anabel didn't understand the subtext implied, she was looking at each person as they fired words across the table like a game of ping-pong and Lucy knew she could start asking questions any moment now.

'Mum, will you just stop!' Lucy hissed.

'What?' Noleen said. 'We're only teasing.'

Kyle held out a cracker to Anabel and she began to pull on it and Lucy was relieved that he had the sense to try and distract her from the conversation the grown-ups were having.

'Come on, Mum!' Mark said, chastising Noleen.

'What?' Noleen said again. 'It's only a bit of fun.'

Lucy pushed back her chair and stood up, tossing her napkin down on the table.

'Are you okay, love?' Pete asked as she walked past him.

'I'm fine, I just want to check on the pudding.' She plastered a smile on her face as she left the room.

In the kitchen she shut the door behind her and allowed herself to rest against it. Tears sprang into her eyes. She knew her mother wasn't being insensitive on purpose but it had stung. Nobody seemed to realise just how upsetting this was for her and there was no quick solution, unless Neil had a change of heart and that wasn't likely anytime soon. She was doing her best to accept it but it was hard on days like this, especially after everything that had happened with Anabel asking Santa for a new baby. It broke her heart that she couldn't give her daughter the one thing she really wanted: a sibling.

After a moment she heard a knock on the door behind her so she quickly wiped her eyes and opened it. It was her mother.

'Oh, love, I'm sorry. I didn't mean to upset you.'

She reached out and put her arm around Lucy's shoulder. 'I was just having a laugh and hoping Neil might finally get the bloody hint.' She didn't disguise the frustration in her tone.

'I told you, Mum, that we've made the decision together.'

'Have you, Lucy? Because it doesn't seem that way to me.'

Lucy knew her mother could see right through her but she couldn't tell her the truth; she'd never understand. 'Yes, Mum, we have. Now c'mon, we'd better get back to the table before they start wondering where we've gone to,' Lucy said.

23

That night, after everyone had gone home, Neil cleaned up the kitchen while Lucy tucked Anabel up in bed. When she returned downstairs, she could tell that Neil was in a huff. He moved around the room in abrupt, jerky movements, slamming cupboard doors too loudly, his footsteps a little too heavy. Even setting Anabel's disappointment with her Santa gifts aside, and after the incident with her mum at the dinner table afterwards, Lucy had actually enjoyed herself. She thought the day had gone well and everyone had seemed to get along. They had played charades after dinner, and she'd kept everyone's wine glass refilled. Her mum and Pamela had been a bit tipsy leaving and Pete, who was the designated driver, had had to escort them into his car.

Lucy pulled out a tea towel from the linen drawer and began drying the last of the pots and pans. She and Neil moved silently around one another; the tension felt thick and girthy. She decided to say nothing. Instead, she left him alone to mull over whatever it was that had worked him up. She wouldn't provoke him by asking if everything was okay; she knew he'd just be snappy.

When they had finished the washing-up and the kitchen was restored to its normal tidy state, he opened the fridge and took out a can of Heineken and sat down with the remote in front of the TV. One of the Bourne movies was playing; Lucy wasn't a fan of action films, so she sat on the armchair and scrolled through her phone, checking out her friends' photos of their Christmases on Instagram. Liking and commenting on their pictures.

She risked a glance across the room at Neil. His jaw was still set in that hard way and his hand was clenched around the tin, as though he was trying to strangle it.

'Is there anything else on?' she asked eventually, growing bored of her phone. Neil had seen these films countless times and there was bound to be something better on TV on Christmas night, something they both could watch.

'What did you tell your mother about us?' he finally said, still keeping his eyes fixed on the screen. She had known there was an argument brewing, and here it was.

'Nothing,' Lucy said, feigning surprise as she looked up from her phone. 'Why?'

'Well, then why was she making all those digs at me during dinner?'

'No, she wasn't. You know what she's like... she just had too much champagne and was a bit giddy.'

'So, you're saying that I imagined it then, is that it?' he continued.

'No, I'm not,' Lucy sighed. 'I'm just saying she didn't mean any harm. You know what that generation is like, sometimes they've no filter; they see Anabel as an only child, and they don't get why we'd choose not to have another baby. Sure, your mum was just as bad. The two of them were as thick as thieves today, getting stuck into the wine.'

Neil shook his head. 'But it was like she knew that it was me who didn't want another baby. She was blaming me. What did you tell her, Lucy?'

There was a dangerous glint in his eyes that told

her she needed to get him off this topic and back onto safer ground. 'I said nothing, I swear,' she lied.

'You're lying to me. I know you've been talking about me behind my back.'

'Neil, calm down, it wasn't like that.'

'So, you did say something then?'

'She asked me recently when we were going to have another baby. She thought we were having trouble getting pregnant, so I told her...' Lucy admitted.

'You told her what?' His tone was as hard and cool as steel.

'I told her that you didn't want another baby,' Lucy stated, knowing as she uttered the words that Neil was going to take them as a personal attack.

'Oh, so you made me out to be the bad guy, is that it?'

'No, Neil, that's not how it went.'

'Well, it certainly felt like that at dinner. There your family were all sitting around *my* table, eating the food that *I* cooked and yet I was made to feel unwelcome – in my own home!'

'C'mon, Neil, it wasn't like that... Sure your mother joined in too. I spoke with Mum in the kitchen and told her it was out of order and that she'd gone too far.'

'I can't believe you told your mum about our private business – something that should only be discussed between us,' he repeated. 'I can't trust you with anything.'

'Neil, please, you have to believe me, it wasn't like that. I've told her that we're both happy with one child and that she needs to stop interfering.'

He shook his head despairingly at her, like she was a small child that he was running out of patience with. 'It's just one thing after another with you lately, Lu.'

His words chilled her. The air in the room had changed and was laced with danger. She knew what would come next if she didn't act quickly. She tried to get away from him but before she could move, he was off the sofa and had made his way across the room. His fist shot out and pounded the side of her jaw. Another punch had landed on her cheekbone before her reflexes even had time to process what had happened. As he pummelled her with his knuckles, she fell off the armchair and slid down to the polished concrete floor. The room began to spin, and pain seared through her. She tried to crawl away from him, but a kick upended her, and she fell flat on the floor. She could taste blood in her mouth. She spat it onto the floor, a red pool forming beneath her face. Neil was standing over her and she saw his boots coming towards her. Her ears were ringing, and she heard herself scream. She tried to put her hands over her head to protect herself, but they kept coming. His boot connected with her abdomen. Her head. Her shoulder. Every part of her until suddenly she didn't feel the pain any more. The agony stopped and everything was peaceful and calm. Beautiful silence descended upon her. She could no longer hear his angry words and the intense ringing in her ears had ceased. She couldn't see his clenched face just inches from hers, with his teeth bared like an animal. She didn't see anything else as everything went dark. She knew that this was it; it was her time to go.

24

Somehow I survived Christmas Day. Despite my bravado to Tim, I had been dreading it. Would I get through it okay or would all the old wounds be re-opened, like a festering cut? Of course I had had my sad moments, especially when I had looked out the window on Christmas morning and seen children on the road cycling new bikes and whizzing along the path on scooters emblazoned with big ribbons with parents looking on warily, warning them to slow down and take their time. I thought back to past Christmases and what might have been if my life had forked down a different path. I felt that familiar lump clot in my throat, the one that could so easily unravel me, but I had learnt a long time ago that you could drive yourself mad with those kinds of thoughts, so I focused on Dora, and we got through the day together.

I kept reminding myself that it was just another day. I told myself that it didn't matter as I peeked out through my curtains and saw that every house on the road had guests going up the path, laden down with gifts, because I had Dora. I had to remember that. I had to admit I might not have fared as well without having the little terrier for company. She had got me through the last few months and given me a reason to feel hopeful again. I might not have a family around me like other people, but I had her and I was grateful she had found me. Tim said I had rescued her, but the truth was, it was she who had saved me. I had to get up in the morning because she had to be fed, I had to leave the house because she had to be walked. She gave me a reason to go on even when all I wanted to do was hide away from the world. I was trying to focus on what I had instead of all I was missing. And it did hurt, especially on days like today; I couldn't help but wonder where they were now. What were they doing?

Could I ever have imagined last year as I sat around the large Formica table in St Jude's that it would be for the last time and that the following year

I would be out on my own in the real world again, living with Dora and on the whole managing pretty well. I had come a long way over the last few months; I knew I wasn't there yet and there was still a long road ahead of me and challenges to be overcome, but I was doing okay.

Dora and I had our usual roast chicken for our Christmas dinner. A turkey would be wasted on us. I had treated myself to a trifle from the refrigerated aisle of the supermarket and Tim had given me a box of mince pies too, which I had been keeping for that night. I thought about Tim and pictured him in England gathered around the table with his new wife and her family all chatting and laughing happily together. Starting their marriage with a clean slate, full of hope and optimism like I once had too. I hoped he was having a good day.

After dinner, I drew the curtains, treated myself to a second mince pie and then myself and Dora settled in to watch TV. *White Christmas* was on and I put a rug over the two of us, relieved that the day had passed and I had got through it. I would be glad to see the back of all the frenzied craziness. People lost the run of themselves in the build-up; I had seen trolleys piled high with food and drink in the supermarket like there would never be a shop open again. Even

Tim, who was always so calm and level-headed, had been like a giddy child when he'd mentioned his Christmas plans to me. I had once been like that too, getting carried away by the madness of it all, I reminded myself. People put so much pressure on one day and expectations could be too high and if your family didn't fit into that perfect Christmas mould, it could be a difficult day. Not everyone had cosy families to spend Christmas with and the disappointment could be crushing when it didn't turn out like the ads on TV. Sometimes people got drunk, tongues were loosened and long-simmering resentments came to the fore. I couldn't wait until January when it would all be over and the world would finally get back to normal. But I was proud of myself all the same.

The film was nearly over and just as the foursome started to croon the title song, I heard shouting coming from next door. Dora heard it too. She sat up and pitched her ears.

I knew it had to be Neil. I felt a shiver chill its way down my body. 'What's going on now, Dora?' I muttered.

I lowered the volume on the TV and listened out. It was definitely a man's voice that was shouting. Could he not leave her alone on Christmas night, I thought. What was wrong with him? He was roaring about something; whatever it was, he wasn't happy. Then there was a bang followed by a scream. Here we go again, I thought. The whole thing was infuriating. Why did Lucy stay with him? Why didn't she just leave him? He was a thug. He was never going to change. How could Lucy be so stupid to think that he might? Then my conscience pricked me; who was I to judge? Things were never as simple as they appeared, I of all people knew that.

I looked at Dora and saw a sheen of fear in her dark eyes.

'What should I do?' I asked her. I felt powerless.

She whimpered in response.

There was another bang and then his voice grew louder until I could just about make out his words.

'...how can I trust you...?'

'...this is all your own fault...'

'Right, Dora, I'll tell you what we're going to do,' I said, standing up and walking out to the hall where the phone was. 'We're going to call the Gardaí and then we're going to have to go in there and try and stop him,' I announced, sounding far braver than I felt. My hand hovered over the phone and I noticed it was trembling. I didn't want to be dragged into this but I couldn't just sit here and listen as Neil battered her either. What if he killed her this time? I couldn't have that on my conscience. I lifted the handset from its cradle and dialled 999.

'It's my neighbour,' I explained to the operator. 'Her husband is going to town on her.'

After I had given her the address, I replaced the handset and exhaled. There was still a lot of noise coming from next door. Surely, he had to come to his senses soon.

'Right, Dora,' I said, inhaling sharply. 'Are you ready?'

Her feet remained planted on the floor.

'I don't want to do this either, old girl, but we don't have much choice,' I said grimly.

I grabbed an umbrella that rested behind the door, thinking it might come in handy as a weapon, then I headed outside into the darkness. I didn't bother putting Dora on the lead as we went next door. I pressed the bell and waited. I was terrified. I didn't know what awaited me inside the house. Would Neil try to assault me too? Let him try, I thought. I'd batter him with my umbrella.

No one answered so I began pounding on the door, hoping that it might disturb him and he might leave poor Lucy alone. Eventually, the door was opened but it was Anabel standing there in the hall. Her eyes were wide with fear and plump tears rolled down her cheeks. She was barefoot and was wearing a little nightdress with a glittery Christmas tree motif. She had a tatty muslin comforter gripped in her hand. A lump formed in my throat at the sight of her.

'Eileen, please tell my daddy to stop,' she whispered. We could still hear Neil's shouts coming from the living room.

'It's okay, love,' I soothed, feeling emotion creep into my own voice at seeing her so distressed. 'You're okay.'

'You stay here,' I instructed Anabel before opening the living room door and bracing myself for what lay ahead. I stepped into the room and saw a lamp and table were upended in the living room; there was blood on the floor and streaking the fabric on the armchair.

Neil was pacing around with his hands clasped behind his head. He hadn't heard me come in yet. I scanned the room and saw Lucy lying unconscious on the floor. Her blonde hair was fanned out around the head. I knew from the angle she was lying at that it wasn't good. I willed the emergency services to hurry on. I wasn't religious, I had lost all faith in God a long time ago, but I found myself praying for him to spare her.

Neil spun around when he heard movement behind him, anger flashing in his eyes. 'What the hell are you doing here?' he asked, charging towards me. I tried to lift the umbrella but my arms wouldn't work. The blood had left my body. I wouldn't be able to take him on; I suddenly realised that I was no match for this man who was almost twice my size, with muscles spilling from his body. I dropped the umbrella and put my hands over my head to protect myself from the blow I knew was coming. Suddenly, Dora growled, then she ran at him and started yapping at his legs, keeping him back from me. He tried to kick her off but she was faster than he was and was able to dodge his attempts.

'It's okay, Dora,' I said. I was afraid she would get hurt but she wouldn't listen to me and kept nipping at his ankles to protect me. I watched Neil's face grow puce, as his frustration with Dora grew.

Moments later, I heard sirens blaring and I could see blue lights strobing around outside. Through the window I saw an ambulance parked on the street behind Neil's car and two paramedics were running up the driveway. Relief washed through me. I watched Neil's face change as he realised what was happening. The angry hardness that had been there just moments ago left him and he crumpled down onto the sofa, holding his head in his hands. I went out into the hall and saw Anabel sitting on the bottom step of the stairs with her legs tucked underneath her chin, looking utterly terrified. I opened the front door to let the paramedics in and pointed towards the living room where Lucy's broken body lay on the floor. Three uniformed Gardaí, one female and two males, quickly followed them into the room. I made my way over to Anabel and sat down on the stairs beside her. 'Are you okay, love?' I asked.

'Is my mammy dead?' she asked me fearfully.

I thought about Lucy's broken body splayed awkwardly on the floor. I didn't know if she was dead or alive. 'The ambulance is here now and it will take her to hospital.'

'But I don't want her to go,' she sobbed, twisting her comforter in her hands.

I held Anabel's hand as two Gardaí emerged from the living room, flanking Neil on either side. They led him out to the squad car.

A few minutes later, the paramedics carried Lucy out of the house on a stretcher. Her head was held in a neck brace and an oxygen mask covered her face. *Thank God*, I thought. *At least she's not dead.*

I stood and watched from the glass pane in the front door as they pushed Neil's head down as he got into the back of the car. Once Lucy's stretcher had been loaded, the ambulance pulled out on to the road and the sirens screeched as it headed towards the hospital. I sat down again beside Anabel on the stairs. I patted the step beside me for Dora to hop up. When Anabel saw Dora, she tried to smile, but the sadness in her eyes was too heavy. And then I did something I wasn't expecting or wasn't sure if I was allowed to do with all the laws and rules around children these days: I pulled her into a hug and let her sob against my body. 'It'll be okay, love,' I whispered.

The female Garda was in the living room examining the scene. I wondered if I should tell her about what had happened the last time. I didn't want to get in anyone's way but I also thought it might be important. I got up from the stairs and made my way in to her.

'Excuse me,' I said as I approached, but she didn't seem to notice me. 'Sorry,' I tried again, louder this time.

She turned around to look at me. 'Can I help you?' she asked. Her eyes travelled along my body from my dressing gown down to my slippers.

'I'm sorry, I know you're busy, but my name is Eileen and I live next door. It was me who called the emergency services. This isn't the first time this has happened, y'know,' I went on.

She turned back around, suddenly taking an interest in me. 'Can I ask you about Mr and Mrs Walsh? Do you know them well?' she probed.

I shook my head. 'Not really. I mean, we're neighbours... but I'm only living here a few months and I keep myself to myself. He hit her a few weeks ago too and their daughter ran next door to get me, the poor child. I tried to get Lucy to report it at the time. Of course, she denied that he had done it, but I knew right well it was him. Beat her black and blue so he did. I should have done something about it myself,' I said regretfully. 'I could have prevented this. It's all my fault.'

'This isn't your fault, Eileen, but I might ask you to drop by the station tomorrow and make a formal statement, if that's okay? My name is Garda Breda McCabe, ask for me.'

I nodded. 'They have a little girl,' I continued, pointing towards the hall. 'Anabel.'

'Yes, I see that. One of our team is informing her next of kin; we're just waiting on them to arrive to take care of her.'

'And then what?'

'Well, hopefully they will be able to look after her until her mother recovers,' Breda stated glumly.

'And if she doesn't? Will you let Anabel go back to that monster?'

'Look, that's not for me to decide. We just have to hope that Mrs Walsh pulls through,' she said solemnly.

The walkie-talkie beeped and Breda talked back and forth to a colleague over the radio.

'We're having difficulty getting in touch with Anabel's grandparents,' she said to me eventually. 'Do you know of any other relatives or friends of the family who we could contact?'

I shook my head. 'As I said, I don't know them well.'

'I really need to get back to the station,' Breda sighed, checking her watch. 'We're really short-staffed with the day that's in it. I'm going to have to take Anabel back there with me.'

I was horrified. A Garda station late at night, full of drunken yobs and criminals, was no place for a child at any time but especially on Christmas night. 'Please don't do that to the child,' I begged. 'She'll be terrified!'

'I don't have a choice, I'm afraid. It's carnage down at the station. The entire team are on call-outs. It's one of our busiest nights of the year.' I could tell by the conversations back and forth across the radio that it was a busy night for the Gardaí, but I couldn't allow Anabel to be brought down there.

'She can stay with me,' I offered in a small voice.

Just then Anabel followed into the living room behind me clutching her cloth comforter, she looked around at the scene, the terror plain in her eyes.

'It's okay, Anabel,' I soothed. She moved closer to me, reached her small hand up towards mine and I encased it in my own.

Garda McCabe eyed me up and I knew she was weighing up the risk. 'Well, we have child-protection considerations to think about... There are normally procedures in place for this kind of situation.'

'Procedures...' I scoffed. 'Half an hour in my house won't do any harm; it'll be a good distraction. I promise I'll take good care of her until her family arrive.'

'She seems comfortable with you,' Breda agreed reluctantly. 'And it would only be for a short while. What do you think, Anabel?' she asked, still sounding unsure.

'Please can I stay with Eileen and Dora?' Anabel begged.

The Garda's radio beeped again, and she took it off the holder to answer it. While she talked over the radio, a moment of panic flitted through me. What if they did some background checks and saw my history? There would be no way that they would leave Anabel in my care if they knew what I was capable of.

'The station has made contact with the child's grandparents and they're on the way apparently...' she announced eventually as she replaced her radio in its holder. 'So, it would only be for a few minutes.'

'Please, Eileen?' Anabel begged, wringing her comforter in between the fingers of her free hand.

I didn't have the heart to disappoint the child. 'Of course you can, love. Will we go inside to my house and get you a hot chocolate?'

Anabel nodded.

My eyes locked on the pool of blood in the middle of the floor, and I shuddered. I said a silent prayer: *Please, God, let Lucy pull through.* 'Come on, let's get out of here.' I steered the child towards the door.

25

Anabel, Dora and I walked up the path to number 26. There was a group of people gathered across the street obviously having come out of their houses to see what all the commotion was about. I kept my head down and didn't make eye contact with any of them as I led Anabel towards my house. The ground sparkled with frost beneath the street lights like someone had sieved icing sugar over the street. On another night, I would have stopped to admire the white-tipped rooftops, but I barely noticed them as I opened the door and led us inside the house.

Anabel was noticeably withdrawn. Her eyes were saucer-like, and her normal chattiness had evaporated. I knew the poor child had got an awful fright. I cursed myself; why hadn't I lodged a complaint against Neil? I should never have listened to Lucy. What had I been thinking? These things were never one-off incidents. Every time I looked at little Anabel, I felt a wave of guilt. I could have prevented this. I couldn't stop my head from wondering, what if the worst happened? What if Lucy didn't pull through? I would never forgive myself. The thought that she might not was unbearable; she had a daughter who needed her.

'Do you want to sit up there, and I'll put on the telly?' I said as we entered the living room.

Anabel climbed up on the sofa and went to sit in Dora's spot. Usually, I wouldn't let anyone sit there but I bit my tongue and left her alone.

'Where is your Christmas tree?' she asked.

'I don't have one.'

Her mouth fell open. 'You don't have a tree? But where did Santa leave your presents?'

'He put them right there on the coffee table,' I said, thinking quickly. I lifted the remote and started flicking through the channels. 'I don't know what's on for kids at this time of the night. What shows do you like to watch on the telly?' I enquired.

Anabel looked at me blankly.

'What do you normally watch on TV?'

'YouTube.'

'I don't have that channel.'

Anabel laughed for the first time that evening and my heart soared. 'It's not a channel. It's an *app*, Eileen,' she explained.

I didn't know what she was talking about, but it was great to see her smile again. 'I see. I don't think I have that.'

'If you don't have it on your TV, I can watch it on your phone,' she suggested.

'I don't have a mobile phone, just a landline.'

Anabel looked at me incredulously. 'You don't have a mobile phone? But how do you send messages or play games?'

I laughed. 'I've more to be doing than playing games.'

I continued flicking through the channels and saw *The Wizard of Oz* was on. 'This will have to do.' I left Anabel and Dora to watch it while I went into the kitchen and made two steaming mugs of hot chocolate. I always kept a jar of cocoa powder in the press for the nights when I couldn't sleep.

When I returned to the living room, Dora was snuggled up on the child's lap. Anabel had her comforter wrapped around her fist and was sucking her thumb.

'You two look very cosy,' I remarked, handing Anabel the cooler mug. I had added extra milk to hers so she wouldn't get burnt.

'What's this movie? It's very strange,' Anabel asked.

'It is a bit odd, all right,' I admitted, 'but I loved it when I was a child.'

Anabel raised the mug to her mouth and took a sip, leaving behind a chocolatey moustache.

'Eileen?'

'Yes, love.'

She turned and locked eyes with me. 'Will my mammy be okay?' So much fear lurked in their depths, and I found myself having to look away from the intensity of her gaze.

'There, there, love,' I soothed. 'Don't be worrying. Of course she'll be okay,' I assured her. 'Doctors and nurses are very clever people. They'll make her better again.' I hated lying to the child because I couldn't promise anything. The truth was that Lucy might not be okay. But what else could I say? Anabel was too young to realise that life could be unbearably cruel sometimes.

'I don't like my daddy any more because he keeps being mean to my mammy.'

My heart ached for this child and the horrors she had witnessed at the hands of her own father.

'Will the police put him in jail?' she continued.

'I'm not sure, love, but they'll be very cross with him.'

Anabel slowly nodded her head. 'That's why Daddy was in handcups.'

I nodded.

'Who's going to mind me now, Eileen?' she asked.

'I'm sure your granny and granddad will be here very soon.'

After half an hour, I saw a car turn into the drive next door and guessed it was probably Lucy's parents. I left Anabel where she was and went outside to talk to them on my own.

'I'm Eileen from next door,' I said, introducing myself as they climbed out of the car. They looked distraught and weary; the worry was etched in every line on their face and I felt such pity for them. What an awful call for a family to get on Christmas night. 'Anabel is over in mine having hot chocolate.'

'Oh, yes,' the man said. 'The Gardaí said you were taking care of her... My name is Pete, and this is my wife, Noleen, we're... eh... Lucy's parents—' His voice choked. 'Thank you very much for looking after her for us.'

I nodded in sympathy. 'Don't mention it. It was my pleasure; she's a great child. I'm so sorry for what you're going through.'

'I still can't believe it,' the woman was saying over and over again. She was staring at number 28 in disbelief, like she couldn't accept what had taken place inside the walls only a short time earlier. 'I just can't believe it.'

The man put his arm around his wife, and she sobbed hard against his chest. 'It's been a huge shock for both of us,' he explained. 'We had no idea that Neil was capable of this.' He shook his head. 'He was like another son to me... How could he do that to her? I trusted him.' His shoulders sagged as he broke down. Once again, I was wracked with guilt; because of my inaction, these people were going through hell right now. I had had the chance to stop it going this far and I'd done nothing.

'Is she okay?' I ventured.

'She's stable. She's in theatre now; they're fixing her arm...' he said, dissolving into tears again. 'It's just such a shock. You live next door to them; did you ever see him doing something like this before?'

'There was an incident a few weeks ago,' I admitted. 'Anabel ran to get me. Other than that, I wouldn't have known a thing. I tried to get Lucy to report it at the time, but she didn't want to go to the Gardaí. I don't know her very well and I didn't want to interfere and so I didn't do anything either...' I trailed off. 'I'm so sorry. I regret not speaking up and telling them, if I had then maybe we wouldn't be in this situation tonight.'

'I should have known,' Noleen said, shaking her head angrily. 'I knew something was wrong, but I thought it was because of something else...'

'You can't blame yourself,' Pete said. 'It was that bastard's fault – God forgive me but that's what he is!' He paused as a sob choked in his throat.

Noleen rubbed his shoulder. 'Come on, love, she's going to be okay. We need to hurry on and get to the hospital.'

Pete composed himself again. 'We're going to bring Anabel to our house and our son Kyle will stay with her while we go to be with Lucy.'

I nodded. 'I'll bring you inside to her.' I led them into my house and hoped they wouldn't judge me on the décor. I wasn't used to having visitors.

'Oh, Anabel,' her grandmother gushed when she saw her and became overwhelmed by tears again. 'What happened to you?'

Anabel started to cry. 'I don't like my daddy any more.'

'Shh, love,' her grandfather soothed, sitting on the sofa beside her.

'Mammy told a lie and said it wasn't Daddy's fault but I knowded that it was.'

'It's all right, love, you don't need to worry about that any more.' Pete pulled the child tight against his chest. 'Come on, we'd better go.'

'Up you get, Dora,' I called. Dora obediently jumped up from Anabel's lap, allowing her to stand.

'Bye, Eileen, thank you for minding me,' Anabel said as they led her out the door.

'You're welcome, love.'

A lump formed in my throat as I watched her through the window getting into her grandparents' car. Anabel had witnessed horrors tonight that no child should ever have to face. I prayed that Lucy would pull through.

26

The last thing Lucy could remember was darkness and she had thought that that was it for her. That this was her time to go. She had heard some people say that they had seen their life flash before them in the moments before they died but Lucy didn't see any of that, she just saw Anabel's tear-stained face, standing at her graveside. A future without a mother and probably a father too. That image wasn't what she wanted for Anabel, and she knew then she couldn't let go. She couldn't just slip away and escape all the pain, like she really wanted to. She had to cling on, claw her way back; she had to fight with every cell in her body to stay here in this world. She wanted to live.

When she woke up next, the room blurred and

swayed around her as if she was on a boat. There were people beside her bed, but she couldn't make out their faces. She tried to lift her head, but it wouldn't move. She raised her arm and saw that it was in a cast. There seemed to be wires trailing her body and her bed was surrounded by high-tech equipment that beeped intermittently.

'Lucy, Lucy,' she could hear a voice saying. It was as if it was down one end of those Talk Tubes that Anabel liked to play with in the playground, and she was at the other. The face moved closer, and she realised it belonged to her dad. Emotion welled up inside her: relief, guilt, fear, it all came flooding out.

'Oh, thank God she's awake.' It was her mother's voice this time and relief warmed Lucy. She was here at her bedside.

'It's okay, take your time, slowly does it,' her dad encouraged.

She tried to nod but everything ached.

'Get the nurse, Pete,' Noleen ordered.

Her father left the room and a minute later returned accompanied by a nurse in blue scrubs. 'Can you hear me, Lucy?' she asked, leaning over and checking her vitals on the monitor. 'Would you like some water?' The nurse held a paper cup to her mouth, and Lucy sipped from it greedily. Her mouth was parched, and her lips crusted with dry skin. 'We're glad to see you awake, I can tell you. You gave us all quite the fright.' She was smiling kindly. 'Would you like me to top up your pain medication?'

Lucy nodded. Everywhere hurt. It all came flooding back to her. How Neil had got angry at her for the way her mother had spoken to him at dinner. Then, before she had even realised what had happened, how he had flown out of his chair and attacked her. How she had fallen to the floor. The hardness on impact. Neil standing over her with his face just inches from hers. The ringing in her ears. The set of his jaw, the grit of his teeth. Then, how the noise had stopped and been replaced with deafening silence as everything had gone dark.

'I'll be back in a minute,' the nurse said, excusing herself. 'Let me get you some more meds.'

Lucy had so many questions that she needed to ask. How had she got here? Where was Anabel now? Had she witnessed what had happened?

'Annie...' was all she managed to get out.

'Don't worry, she's okay,' her dad said, giving her hand a tight squeeze.

Lucy started to panic. Her parents might not know it was Neil who had put her here. That he was dangerous. If he was in the house with Anabel and was still in a temper, he could hurt her. She tried to sit up in the bed, but she couldn't pull herself up. 'Neil...' she tried.

'Just relax, love. You're safe now, you don't need to worry about anything. Neil is in the Garda station where scumbags like him belong. Kyle is minding Annie in our house until we get home.'

She allowed herself to relax down onto the pillows again, feeling shame scald her. The secret that she had tried to keep hidden for so long was out there. They knew. They all knew that Neil had done this to her. Her own husband. There were no more lies or excuses she could tell them. The police must have been involved if Neil was at the Garda station. She was frightened. Neil would blame her. He would be furious when he saw her; he hated people interfering in their business and now her parents had done the worst thing possible and got the Gardaí involved. *Why had they called the Gardaí*, she wanted to ask. *Could they not have left them to deal with this themselves?* Neil could end up with a criminal record because of this. If word got out, his business could be ruined. They had handled this all wrong. She felt a sinking sense of dread.

'You're lucky to be here, Lu; you've a broken arm,

broken ribs, a broken nose and a fractured eye socket.'
Pete shook his head.

Her father's words walloped her. Neil – the same
man who promised he loved her endlessly – had done
this to her. He had promised her after the last time
that it would never happen again. He had sworn on
Anabel's life, and she had believed him. She felt embarrassed and naïve for allowing this to happen.

'He's a monster!' Noleen sobbed.

'He had us all fooled,' her father echoed bitterly.
'He'd better hope I never set eyes on him again...'

'You should have told us, love. We could have
helped you!' Noleen choked back tears but, despite
her upset, her voice was tinged with anger. 'Why
didn't you say something?'

Lucy felt so guilty for bringing this drama to her
parents' door. They were in their sixties; it was time
for them to be relaxing and enjoying life, not worrying about their grown-up daughter. She was also
embarrassed for letting herself get into this mess. Her
parents had raised her to be strong and independent
and look how she had ended up.

'Leave it for now, Noleen,' Pete soothed, 'we've
plenty of time for all of that. What matters now is that
she's alive.'

27

The days between Christmas and New Year ticked by slowly. I was keeping an eye on the house next door and hadn't seen a soul coming or going. I still didn't know how Lucy was. I had called into the Garda station on St Stephen's Day and given a statement to Garda McCabe as she had requested. I had asked if she knew how Lucy was doing but she said she didn't have an update on her condition. I didn't have contact details for Lucy's parents, and I knew that because I wasn't a relative, the hospital wouldn't give me any information on her condition if I tried calling them. Besides, I didn't even know what hospital she was in. I prayed that she had pulled through. I thought about little Anabel too; I hoped the child was doing all right.

Dora and I carried on as best we could. I was relieved that the pressure of Christmas was finally over. The weeks of build-up felt like a bottle of fizzy coke that had been shaken too much that when you twisted the lid, you didn't know how much was going to come out, but we had survived the madness and I was proud of myself for getting through it all relatively unscathed. The ads of cosy families gathered around a dinner table and little children getting excited as they unwrapped presents had disappeared from the TV, and normality was slowly being restored once more.

One day I was watching telly when I saw a car turn into the driveway next door. I hadn't seen anyone going in or out of there since Christmas night. I moved closer to the net curtains and saw Lucy's father getting out of the car. I hurried outside with Dora trotting after me.

'Hi there,' I called over the wall. I noticed that he didn't look as distraught as he had on the first night that I had met him, when he had been ashen with shock and worry.

He turned from where he was putting the key in to open the front door. 'Oh, hello,' he replied, making his way over towards me.

'I just wanted to ask how Lucy is doing? She's been on my mind all Christmas.'

'She's doing well, thank you. She's still in hospital and she has a lot of broken bones but at least bones heal.'

'Oh, thank God,' I exhaled heavily. 'I've been worried sick thinking about her.'

'It was touch and go there for a while but she's a fighter...' He paused. 'You know, she was born two months premature. She weighed the same as a bag of sugar. We used to go watch her lying in the incubator, all tubes and wires coming out of her, and I would say to Noleen, she's strong that one, but I never imagined she'd be proving it to us in this way.' His bottom lip trembled.

'I can imagine. The main thing is that she's on the mend. And little Anabel, how is she?'

'She's good, thank you. She's missing her mum, of course, but the good news is that Lucy is being released tomorrow. That's why I'm here, actually; I want to give the place a tidy-up, get the heating on so that the house is nice and warm for her before she comes home.'

'That's a lovely idea. What about Neil?' I asked, wondering what had become of him. I hoped he was locked up somewhere. An animal like him deserved to be in a cage.

Peter sighed. 'He was released. Lucy doesn't want to press charges. A file is being sent to the DPP to see if charges can be brought that way but without a statement from Lucy, it weakens the case against him.'

I couldn't believe what I was hearing. 'Why on earth won't she press charges?' I asked sharply. I know it was none of my business, but I just couldn't understand it. 'After what he did to her? She could have died!' What was she thinking? It wasn't the first time it had happened. Lucy couldn't just let him get away with it.

Pete shook his head. 'Beats me. You think you know someone... I trusted him; I thought he was a good husband and father... After what he did, I want them to lock him up and throw away the key but Lucy's thinking of Anabel, you see. He's her dad and if he serves time in prison or has a criminal record, she's worried about how it might affect her down the line.'

I grimaced. 'I suppose it's not black and white, is it?' I agreed. 'So where is he staying now then?'

'With his mother, apparently.'

'Lucy's not going to let him come back here, is she?' I asked.

Pete shook his head. 'Over my dead body. I never want to see sight nor sound of that fella again.'

Despite Pete's words, I wondered if Neil would have the audacity to force his way back into the house when he heard Lucy was home. I wouldn't put it past him.

'The courts have put a barring order in place and I've a locksmith coming out shortly to change the locks,' Pete continued as if reading my mind.

'Good thinking. I can keep an eye on things too.'

'Thank you, Eileen, we'd appreciate that. We wanted her to come stay with us for a while until she's back on her feet again but she wouldn't hear of it. She wants Annie back at home where she belongs so between myself, Noleen and the boys, we will take turns staying with her here for a while anyway.'

'She's lucky to have a family like that.'

'We're all just so grateful that she's alive.' He paused. 'I don't think I thanked you properly for taking Annie in that night and for going to Lucy's assistance the time before. You're a good neighbour.'

'That's what neighbours are for,' I mumbled, the compliment taking me unawares.

'Right, I'd better get a move on here. See you, Eileen.'

'Bye,' I said. 'Come on, Dora.'

As I returned to my own house, warmth filled my heart. It had been a long time since I'd felt useful. I was so used to being a burden or being the one that other people had to look after but I had done something that had helped another person, and it felt good to be appreciated.

28

Lucy took a deep breath as she entered the house. She made her way down the hallway, then as she went into their open-plan living area, stopped to rest for a moment. She looked around the room. There was no sign of what had happened here just a few days earlier. The place looked pristine, even tidier than it normally would be. Lucy guessed her parents had probably cleaned it before she came home. Her eyes roved across the living area, to the armchair that she had been sitting on just moments before Neil's outburst, not realising how quickly her world was about to turn upside down. She noticed a rust-coloured stain on the upholstery that hadn't been there before and the glass candleholder that normally sat on the coffee table was missing; she presumed it had got smashed during the drama but that was the only clue about what had happened.

'How about a cuppa, love?' Noleen suggested, following in behind her with Anabel and Pete.

'Thanks, Mum.'

Pete helped her to sit down on the sofa. Despite the high doses of painkillers that she was on, everywhere hurt. 'Easy does it, love,' he said, guiding her down gently.

'Where's Daddy, Mammy?' Anabel was looking warily around the room, and Lucy knew she was anxious about coming home.

Noleen's eyes darted over to Lucy, wondering how she was going to explain it to the child.

She took a deep breath. 'He's staying with Granny Pamela, love,' she said, hoping that that explanation wouldn't lead to more questions.

Anabel visibly relaxed before her eyes, clearly relieved to hear that her dad wasn't coming home. She ran over to play with her toys and Noleen exchanged a look with Pete.

When Noleen had made the tea, she brought over the mug and put it on the little glass-topped circular side table beside Lucy. 'There you go, love.' She took the throw off the back of the sofa and put it across her daughter's knees.

Pete followed Anabel over to her play area and helped her to set up a house using cushions from the sofa. As Lucy sipped her tea, she watched them. Anabel was enjoying have someone to play with and was giggling as Pete put on a princess crown and started talking in a girlish voice: 'I'm pwincess Peterelle and you are my servant Stinkybelle.'

'Lucy,' Noleen began hesitantly, sitting down beside her on the sofa. 'Pamela called me earlier.'

Lucy's breath stalled in her chest. 'What did she want?'

'She wanted to see how you were doing.'

Lucy put the mug back down on the coaster. She had been thinking about Neil a lot over the last few days. He had sent her several messages which she hadn't replied to. They all said versions of the same thing, that he was so sorry. That he was a monster. That he was disgusted with himself. That he wanted to talk whenever she was ready. That he promised he would engage with counselling properly. They would have to talk eventually; she knew that much. She couldn't hide from Neil and her marriage forever and, besides, she had questions that she wanted to ask him and the biggest one of all was: why? Why did he have to do this to them? They had a great life; why did he have to throw it all away? Did she mean so little to him that his temper was stronger than his love for her?

'How is he?' she asked. She wondered if he was as upset as she was. She had to bear the physical pain, but did he regret what he had done to her, to Anabel, to their family?

'She said he's in a bad place.'

Lucy nodded. 'Well, that makes two of us.'

'It's no more than he deserves! Pamela said that he wanted to see you face to face. Apparently, he wants to say sorry for what happened and that he's missing you and Anabel. I told her that this was all his own doing and that it was too late for remorse now. I think Pamela was trying to sound it out with me, to see if you'd be open to meeting up to talk with him but I told her in no uncertain terms that you never want to see him again. Neil is not to set foot here in this house ever again.'

Lucy felt herself bristle. 'Mum, you can't make that decision for me.'

'What?' Noleen was outraged. 'You're going to let him come here and listen to whatever bullshit he wants to feed you?'

'No, Mum, I don't know what I'm doing, to be honest... my head is a mess... but just stop interfering and let me figure it out myself.'

Noleen shook her head. 'I can't believe I'm hearing this after what he did!'

'It's not that simple; we're married. He probably misses Anabel. All his stuff is here.'

'Are you trying to defend him?'

Disturbed by the raised voices, Anabel glanced across to the sofa to see what was going on. Lucy smiled at her reassuringly, so she knew that everything was okay, and she went back to playing.

'No, Mum, I don't know what I'm doing,' she said quietly. She felt so confused by it all. She was so split in her feelings. She was angry, but she missed him. She knew she should hate him, but she didn't. She wanted to defend him, but she also knew his actions were indefensible. She wanted to be loyal to her husband, but she knew that he had lost all rights to loyalty when he had first attacked her. How could she reconcile the two parts of her that hated what he had done to her and Anabel, but still loved him? Her job was to protect her daughter, but she never thought she'd have to protect her from her own father. She was like a rolled-up pair of socks being separated; she was being torn apart from the inside out. She felt so conflicted – yes, he had done a bad thing, but he wasn't a bad person.

The worst part of it all was that this wasn't the man she loved. This wasn't him. He was normally loving and kind. When she had been pregnant with Anabel, he wouldn't let her lift a finger. She hadn't cooked or cleaned for nine months; he had done it all. Or whenever she had a long day in work, she would come home to find a hot bath waiting for her to climb into. How could Lucy reconcile the two versions of the same man? He had made a terrible mistake and now instead of being able to fix the problem themselves, it had spread further out, like ripples from a stone cast into water – the problem had grown.

Lucy didn't want her parents watching over her like she was some sort of overgrown child. She wanted her old life back, but it had been snatched away from her and the person responsible for that was the very person she missed most. It pained her that he had done this, that he was the reason they were now apart. Lucy didn't know what the future held for their marriage; how could they possibly move on from here? Her parents expected her to hate him, but she didn't hate him – she loved him despite everything, and she knew that he loved her. Sometimes though, love wasn't enough. Lucy knew it would have to be over her parents' dead bodies if she tried to take him back. She wasn't even sure if she wanted him back, but she longed for her old life before everything had gone wrong. They had been so happy, they had had Anabel, they had renovated their dream home, they both had jobs they loved and then, *pop*, like somebody had stuck a pin in a balloon, it had all disappeared. How Lucy wished she had never brought up the idea of having another baby. Could she have avoided all this heartache? She would never know the answer to that question. Wasn't she allowed to be sad or feel uncertain? She was grieving the loss of her fairy tale and also the fact that the vows they had exchanged, full of hope and optimism, had been shattered.

And now their families were involved. The Gardaí too. Probably the whole street knew their business and maybe even the whole community would too if the local newspaper covered it in their weekly court section.

'There's a barring order in place so if you let him back here at all, he'll be breaking the law,' Noleen reminded her with a wagging finger as though Lucy was still five years old and had been caught trying to steal a biscuit from the tin.

'All right, Mum, I get it!' Lucy knew there was no

point in trying to get her to listen. Her mother came from a long line of strong Dublin women, and she wasn't afraid to share her opinion. She had always been overbearing and it seemed that since her time in hospital, she was doubly so.

'Come on, love.' She took Lucy's hand in her own. 'I need you to see this for yourself. Do you have any idea of the fright we got that night to have the Guards knock on our door? To be told the news that you were in a serious condition in hospital and then after all of that to learn that it was Neil – the man we trusted like a son – who had put you there? Think of how you would feel if it were Anabel. Could you imagine getting a call like that in the future?' Noleen was getting choked up. 'We nearly lost you, Lu; I won't let him do it for real next time.'

'I know, Mum,' Lucy said contritely, the guilt catching her. She felt guilty for everyone. Guilty for Anabel and everything she had seen. Guilt for her parents and the worry they were enduring. Guilt for dragging everyone into this mess. So much guilt. 'I just feel so lost. I don't know where to start. I've been with Neil since I was fourteen; that's over half my life. I don't know myself without him. He's Lucy's father – we own this house together – everything, my whole life, is connected with his.' She didn't know how to live her life without Neil in it. She didn't *want* to live her life without him.

'You don't need to start anywhere. We'll take it day by day, hour by hour, if we have to. Right now, you have your family all around you, you just need to concentrate on getting better again for Anabel's sake. We'll worry about the bigger stuff down the line.'

29

I had watched from the window as Lucy arrived home from hospital. Her arm was in a cast and her battered face was barely recognisable as she came up the path flanked by her father, while her mother helped Anabel out of the car. Once again, I had felt fury rise within me for what her husband had done to her.

I had decided to let them settle in before calling over later that evening to see how she was doing. I normally didn't do things like this; I wasn't the kind of neighbour to drop round for a coffee and chat; I always kept myself to myself, but something wouldn't rest inside me. Perhaps it was because I had seen her at her most vulnerable on two occasions now or maybe it was because she reminded me of my younger self, but I felt a responsibility towards her that I couldn't explain. I wanted to let her know that I was there for her. If she needed any help she could always knock on my door.

Later that evening, Dora and I stood outside number 28 and pressed the doorbell. It was Lucy's mother who answered.

'Hi Noleen, I just wanted to see how Lucy was doing?'

'Eileen,' she said in surprise. 'I didn't get to thank you properly for everything that you did for us. We really do appreciate it.'

'That's what neighbours do,' I mumbled. 'It wasn't nice for anyone. Least of all Lucy and little Anabel.'

'I blame myself, y'know?' Noleen sucked in sharply and I could see she was on the verge of tears. These last few days must have been so distressing for her. I wondered if Neil ever thought about that. Did he realise how far-reaching his actions were? So many people's lives had been destroyed by what he had done.

'Sure, how could you blame yourself?' I asked.

'I should have noticed something was off with her. She told me that she really wanted to try for another baby but himself wouldn't hear of it. That day at Christmas dinner, I was giving him a few digs about it all. I-I'd had a couple of glasses of wine,' she admitted sheepishly. 'I-I meant it as a joke, but I should have seen that he was getting worked up by it all. Then all hell broke loose after we went home. I had no idea that he was capable of doing something like this.'

'Neil is a monster; no one else can be blamed for his actions.'

Noleen grimaced and nodded. 'Anyway, come in out of the cold.'

'Ah no, I don't want to be intruding, I just wanted to check she was okay.'

'Please, Eileen, Lucy would like to see you,' Noleen begged. 'You'd be a good distraction for her.' She sighed. 'Heaven knows she's sick of the sight of me. Everything I say seems to be wrong...'

'Well, I won't stay long then,' I conceded, stepping into the house.

Noleen did a double take as Dora followed me inside, but I pretended not to notice. We come as a pair; where I go, she goes. Noleen led us down the hall and opened the door leading to the living area.

'Lucy, Eileen is here to see you,' she said.

I saw her sitting on the sofa, wrapped in a big fleecy dressing gown; her hair was tied back in a messy ponytail and dirty-yellow bruising marred her pretty face. Dark shadows, which I wasn't sure were from tiredness or bruises, hung like moons beneath her eyes.

'Dora!' Anabel cried, jumping up from where she was watching TV and running over to pet her.

'Eileen!' Lucy said, clearly surprised to see me in her living room. 'I'm glad you're here. I wanted to thank you for your help the other night and, well... you know...'

'Don't mention it. I'm just glad you're okay. How are you feeling?' I asked.

'Still quite sore.'

'Sit down,' Noleen instructed. 'Can I make you a cuppa?'

'No thanks,' I said, wanting to keep the visit brief. If I got stuck drinking tea, then I'd never get out of there. Anabel was rubbing Dora's belly and the little terrier's leg was twitching as she tickled her.

'You have to have a cuppa, it's the least I can do.' Noleen set to filling the teapot with water directly from the hot water tap and I knew there would be no telling her otherwise.

We sat down and sipped the tea that Noleen made, making polite chit-chat until Anabel let out a large yawn. She had her ragged comforter wrapped around her hand and her thumb stuck in her mouth.

'I'd better get you ready for bed, young lady,' Noleen said. 'You're exhausted.'

'No, I'm not!'

'Go on, Annie,' Lucy cajoled, 'Granddad is upstairs filling the bath for you. You go up with Nana and then I'll be up shortly to do your story.'

'Okay, Mammy,' she sighed as she gave Dora one last rub before she stood up from the floor. 'Goodnight, Eileen. Goodnight, Dora.'

'Goodnight, Anabel,' I called after her. 'It's good to see you home where you belong,' I said to Lucy after Anabel had disappeared upstairs with her grandmother. 'How's Anabel doing?'

'She got a fright.'

Now that we were alone, there was something I needed to say to her. I took a deep breath. 'Look, I know we don't know each other well and you can tell me to mind my own business if you want but you can't let Neil come back here.'

She drew back from me. I knew she thought I had overstepped the mark and was interfering, but I didn't care. I wanted her to understand how important this was.

'You can't let it happen again,' I repeated. 'For Anabel's sake.'

'I know that.' There was a defensive edge to her tone.

'Because he'll do it again and the next time you might not wake up.'

Lucy's gaze fell to the floor, and I knew she had the very same fears.

'You remind me of myself, you know,' I continued.

She looked up at me and met my eyes. Her brows were raised in scepticism, and I guessed she was probably insulted that I would compare myself to her. In her eyes we had nothing in common.

'No, really,' I continued, unperturbed. 'I was once just like you. I had it all too.' I hadn't come here to share my own story with her but, sitting here beside her, I knew I had no choice. I needed her to see what she was doing. That she had an opportunity now to change the course of her life for the better; she just had to be strong and reach out for it. Yes, the unknown was always scary but if she slipped back down the familiar, well-worn path because it was easier, then I was sure she wouldn't live to tell the tale. I needed her to listen to me.

30

Lucy's face searched mine and I knew I had got her attention.

'Go on,' she encouraged, clearly intrigued.

I took a deep breath to steady myself, knowing that where I was about to go wasn't going to be easy. 'Well, I was once married. I had two children.'

I saw disbelief cross over her face. 'You were?' she spluttered. 'What happened to them?'

It had been years since I had spoken about them and, even then, it was only in the safe space of the counsellor's office or with Tim. Was I ready to pull back the lid on that part of my life and unleash all the feelings and emotions that for so long I had managed to keep trapped inside? But there was a vulnerability in Lucy's eyes that I recognised. I didn't know her well, but I felt as though I could see into her soul. There was something in Lucy that I could identify with. She had triggered me into opening up to her. I couldn't just stand by and watch her lose everything like I had. Even though I knew it would be far easier to stay safe inside the walls of my own house, just shut the door on Lucy and Anabel and their problems and forget all about this, my conscience wouldn't let me do it. I wanted her to understand what could happen and all that was at stake. While our circumstances were different, she didn't realise how slowly these things could start out, how quietly they crept up on you. One day you feel like you're going through a rough patch and then the next, everything seems bleak, and you think you've no way out. I didn't want Lucy to go through the same thing as I had and lose everything. She had a chance to save herself; how I wished someone had done the same for me once upon a time.

'Well, I found it hard to cope after my first child Liam was born,' I began. 'He was a difficult baby, and he cried a lot. I couldn't get him to stop no matter what I did. I hated going anywhere with him because every time I left the house he would cry even more.

He'd cry if I stayed at home too, but at least there was no one to see it. I was afraid that people were looking at me and judging me, so I stopped going places. Everything overwhelmed me. I couldn't mind Liam and keep the house clean or make dinner. Dan, my husband, would come from work to find the dirty washing still piled up beside the washing machine, there would be no dinner ready, not even a slice of bread to be found in the bread bin. I knew by the sigh of frustration when he was faced with bare cupboards once again after a long day in work, that he was losing patience. Anyways, I fell pregnant again and we had Eoghan. There were only sixteen months between my sons – *Irish twins*, I called them. Then I really struggled. Dan didn't get it, he was working full-time, I was on maternity leave from my job in the bank, so I was at home with the children. He did his job, and he couldn't understand why I couldn't just do mine like I was supposed to. That was the deal. I was supposed to get on with it while he earned the money. My family all lived in Cork and the few friends that I had, I made excuses not to see. I was terrified that everyone would judge me. I couldn't manage the babies; I was severely sleep-deprived. I would finally get one to sleep and try to get some sleep myself, then the other would wake up. Or I'd be feeding one and the other would cry to be fed too. It felt like someone was always cry-ing. The more I got upset about letting everything get on top of me, the worse it became. Then Dan would come in the door after a long day in work and start having a go at me because the place was a tip.'

'Didn't he try help you out a bit?' Lucy asked.

'He did what he could, but he didn't understand why I couldn't just get on with things. He said he'd love to be at home all day living it up on maternity leave instead of dealing with eejits in work. Anyway, things kept getting worse and I was constantly doubting myself. I couldn't remember doing things. I would wonder if I had fed the babies or when I had last washed them. I stopped eating but I was never hungry. I thought things were moving in the house too. I had a pile of pictures left in the hallway that I had been meaning to hang, and then one day they were up on the wall. Dan said that he didn't put them up and I didn't remember doing it either. I couldn't trust my own mind. Then one weekend, he sent me to Cork to see my family. He said I could use the break. Despite everything, I missed them all. I decided to get an early train home on Sunday but when I got back to the house, there was a woman I didn't know there. She was holding my baby, bouncing him on her knee and he was giggling at her. As I stood there looking at them, it all looked so perfect. Like they were meant to be the family, and I was the outsider. As soon as she saw me the woman handed the baby over to Dan and jumped up from the sofa. Dan seemed flustered as he introduced her and explained that they worked together. She said a hasty goodbye, before hurrying out the door. After she had left, I asked him if they were together and he told me I was being ridiculous, that she had just been dropping off a file for work. He said it was insulting to both of them that I would imply there was anything more going on between them. But I became convinced that they were having an affair although he always denied it and told me I was crazy. Even now to this day, I don't know what was true or untrue from that time.'

'Didn't your husband see that you were struggling?' Lucy asked. 'Didn't he try to get you help?'

'He did his best, but he couldn't understand it. I know it wasn't that long ago but even back then there was such ignorance around mental health. He kept telling me to pull myself together. He would compare me to other people we knew who had had a baby at the same time and were managing just fine: a friend, a neighbour, his sister. He'd say, "Look at so-and-so up the road, they had a baby last month and they're able to get out and about with the pram. Why can't you be like that?" And I couldn't answer because I wondered the same thing myself – *what was wrong with me?* Why was I the only woman struggling? Why did I find it so hard when every other mother made it look so easy? Then one day I met a friend of ours, Ruth McKeever, in the supermarket. Liam was throwing a tantrum and Eoghan was crying in his pram, and I just wanted to throw myself down on the floor and cry too. Anyway, Ruth lifted Eoghan up from the pram and of course he instantly stopped crying for her. I headed home, feeling like even more of a failure. Dan came home from work that evening and said that Ruth had called him at work, saying she was worried about me. He had another go at me again about pulling myself together. He said it was embarrassing, and that people were starting to gossip about me; he said I was the talk of the town. That just made me feel even worse about myself.'

'It sounds like you had postnatal depression,' Lucy said gently.

I nodded. 'I think I probably had, but I didn't realise it. I had heard people talking about the "baby blues", that it was normal and would pass in a few weeks, but this didn't feel normal. It never got better and no one else seemed to be struggling as much as I was.'

'It sounds horrible and so lonely for you to go through that on your own. So, what happened next?' Lucy asked, riveted by the story.

'Well, one day I found myself on the street in my pyjamas. A neighbour who knew me brought me home, but I was very confused and disorientated. I had left the babies in the house on their own. They were both fine, but it frightened me that I didn't remember doing it or even why I had left them. The neighbour rang Dan at work and told him he had better come home. Dan left work early, but he wasn't happy. We ended up having a huge argument. He told me I should make an appointment with my doctor.'

'And did you?'

I shook my head. 'I couldn't do it. Even that seemed overwhelming. That's how bad things were. Everything spiralled after that. It had got to the stage where I didn't want to live. I was a burden on Dan. I thought the boys would be better off without me. I was a failure as a mother – my babies deserved far more than I was able to give. I was a failure as a wife; Dan was under pressure in work, and I was just adding to his stress by not being able to manage the home side of our life. One day I was driving the roads trying to get the babies to sleep; it was the only time where they'd both sleep together. I found myself at a lake. I don't know where it was or how I got there or even what I was doing there. The water was so still and calm like a sheet of steel glinting under the sunlight. I drove up to the water's edge and it looked so tranquil and serene. So inviting. I knew I could end it and escape this torment. My family didn't need me, I was a liability. I was a pathetic mother to the boys, and they'd be better off without me.'

'So, what did you do?' Lucy asked, her eyes wide.

I closed my eyes and I was back there again, the cool sweat prickling the back of my neck, the sense of temptation to immerse myself in that water and be rid of all the pain stronger than any other feeling inside me. The tears rolling down my cheeks. The boys dozing in the back seat. My foot heavy on the accelerator. *Go on*, a voice said, *keep going; this will all be over soon.* 'Well, the car hit a crop of reeds at the edge of the water, and I had to press harder to get the car to drive over them. My eldest Liam woke up with the revving of the engine. He started to cry and it jolted me. I looked behind me at my two babies strapped into the back seat and knew I couldn't do it to them.

They deserved more. I got out of the car and lifted Eoghan out in his car seat and brought it up the shore away from the water. I unstrapped Liam and led him to where I had left his brother. Then I kissed their silky heads for the last time and told them that I loved them more than they would ever understand but they deserved better than me. I told Liam to wait there and mind his brother. He wasn't yet three, but he understood what I was saying. When I turned around to make sure he wasn't following me towards the water, he did what he was told and stayed with his brother.

'You just left them there?' Lucy was clearly horrified. 'Two small boys. At the edge of a lake?'

I nodded. 'I told you that I wasn't able to take care of them,' I said sharply. 'I continued down to the water, filled my pockets with the stones that lay along the shore and walked in. The biting shock of the cold water is the last thing I remember.'

Lucy, who was clearly at a loss for words, gasped and I wondered if I had told her too much. I knew I had shocked her but that was what I'd wanted. I had to make her see what could happen when you hit rock bottom. She needed to understand that our lives weren't as different as she had once thought; that the link between our happiness and mental health was as delicate as a thread.

'So... so, what happened then? Why didn't you drown?' she asked.

'I believe a couple who were out walking saw me go in. The wife ran to the boys, and her husband followed me into the cold water, fully clothed, and dragged me out. I wouldn't be here today if it wasn't for his bravery and I don't even know who they are. I never got to thank them. When I think about it now, I hate myself. How could any mother abandon two small children at the side of a lake? I don't even recognise myself.'

'You weren't well. It wasn't you that was doing it, it was the illness.'

I nodded. 'I've had a lot of therapy over the years, and I've learnt to separate the illness from myself but, even still, I find it inconceivable that I could do that. Anything could have happened to the boys; Liam might have followed me down to the water... He could have wandered up on to the road and been hit by a car... Someone could have kidnapped them. All kinds of horrible things could have happened to them, and I, their mother, who was supposed to nurture and protect them, was too ill to see it because I selfishly only cared about ending my own pain.'

'What happened next?' Lucy asked in a whisper.

'Well, I spent a week in hospital being treated for

the effects of near drowning. From there I was transferred to a psychiatric hospital.'

'How long were you there for?'

'Almost two months.'

'Were you allowed to go home then?'

I shook my head vigorously. 'How could I go home after what I had done? And besides, even if my family had accepted me back, I wouldn't have gone anyway. I lost all rights to my home on the day I decided to do what I did.'

'So where did you go?' Lucy was enthralled.

'I went to a step-down facility called St Jude's. It was like the hospital but smaller. It was supposed to be a stepping stone between the hospital and going back into the community, but I liked it there. I felt safe. It might sound strange, but it became my new home. I spent almost ten years there.'

'What happened to your family? Didn't you ever see them again?' Lucy was aghast. 'Did your husband not come to visit you or your family from Cork or even your friends?'

I shook my head. 'Why would they? Everyone was horrified by what I had done. My parents did try to visit several times over the years, but I refused to see them. Even though I knew they were after driving the whole way up from Cork, I always told the staff to send them home. I never saw any of them again.'

'Didn't your husband at least try to contact you?'

I shook my head again. 'No and I don't blame him. What I did was unforgiveable. I didn't deserve to see my family again.'

'But your children, surely you saw them again?' Lucy asked in disbelief.

I shook my head. 'I told you; I never saw anyone again after that day.'

Tears filled Lucy's eyes. 'That's just so sad. I can't imagine...' She trailed off.

I looked out at the garden where beyond the glass a little bird fluttered down, pecked at the ground for a moment before taking off again. 'That's life, isn't it?' I shrugged. 'It doesn't always turn out the way we plan.'

'So how did you end up here on St Brigid's Road?'

'Well, once I began showing signs of recovery, they were always trying to get me to leave St Jude's. Once you begin getting better, they don't want patients clogging up beds. They tried many times to get rid of me, but I wouldn't go. "The only way I'll be leaving this place is in a six-foot box," I used to tell them when they started at me again. Where would I have gone? I'd have been homeless. And besides, I didn't want to. So, whenever they brought up the subject of leaving,

I'd start acting up. Normally, I was a very well-be-haved patient but suddenly I'd become uncooperative or stop taking my meds or whatever it took, so they'd back off and leave me alone. They were always afraid of putting too much pressure on the patients in case we spiralled again. Then Tim started working there – he's my key worker – and I liked him. He always had a smile on his face, and none of the staff ever seemed to smile in there. Tim had time for everyone; he was never too busy to stop for a chat. He would listen to our concerns, not like some of the rest of them working there, who wouldn't so much as look you in the eye. I felt that he understood me and could per-haps see a glimmer of the woman I used to be, before it all went wrong. Even though he too was always banging on at me about leaving St Jude's to live inde-pendently, he had a nice way of doing it. Anyways, eventually Tim talked me round, and convinced me to give it a go. They got me this place and helped me to settle in. They told me to give it a couple of weeks and if I didn't like it, I could go back to St Jude's. Tim checked in with me every day, even when he was sup-posed to be off; he'd give me a call to see how I was, that's the sort he is. On my first night out of St Jude's I didn't think I'd last the night. I rang Tim from my bed, terrified. The noises were different, it was too quiet, there was no one pacing the corridor and no trolley rattling with crockery after teatime. My bed was much bigger too and everything was strange, but he answered the phone and calmed me down. He told me I was doing great. I stuck it out for Tim's sake; you see, he's so nice that you just don't want to let him down. And then Dora came into my life just after I moved in, and it was nothing short of a miracle. I knew I couldn't go back to St Jude's and leave her behind. Dora gave me a reason to stay. I don't think I'd have lasted this long without her.'

'Wow, I-I had no idea about any of this, Eileen.'

I nodded. 'It's pretty wild all right,' I quipped.

'Where are they now – your family?'

'Well, my parents died when I was in St Jude's. I never went to their funerals.'

'I'm so sorry to hear that. What about your husband and sons?'

'I honestly don't know. We lived in village of Carlingford in County Louth back then but I don't know whether they stayed there or if they have moved somewhere else.'

'Didn't you ever try and visit your old home and see if they still live there?' Lucy suggested.

I looked at her as though she was crazy. 'I told you I lost all rights to knowing them on the day I almost killed them. They're better off without me. It wouldn't be fair on them to knock on their door and upset them all over again.'

'Couldn't you ask Tim about your family and how they are now?' Lucy suggested. 'Even if you never went near them, at least you'd know what happened to them. You'd have some closure.'

'I purposely haven't. I don't want to know. What good would come of it? I'd just be torturing myself. I'm better off focusing on getting through each day. If I start thinking about all of that, it's too painful. The past belongs in the past.'

'What if you were to bump into them on the street one day?'

I felt a chink appear in my bravado. If I was honest, there wasn't a day that went by when I didn't worry about the same thing myself. Ireland was a small place. I had already bumped into Ruth McKeever; how long would it be until I met Dan or one of the boys? For all I knew I could already have walked past them in the street and not even known. They were teenagers now and soon they would be finished school and could move out of home. They could move to this street, and I wouldn't even know. I had tried telling myself that of course I'd recognise my own flesh and blood. Surely, something inside me, the strong maternal bond, that thing that made me a mother, would help me recognise my own offspring, but as the years went by, I wasn't so sure. All I had now were the chubby-cheeked memories of them and even those I couldn't trust. I guessed their plump baby faces would have sharpened into the angular features of teenagers by now. I wondered if they were fair-skinned like me or if they took after their father with his dark features? I would try to imagine what they might look like now; I would picture them as babies and what they would look like as young men, but I could never do it. Would their hair still be long, with soft baby curls delicately brushing their necks, or would the curls have been cut into a tight hairstyle? I realised it was impossible to imagine what they had turned out like. It made me sad to think that I could walk past them on the street and not even realise. That's why I never went anywhere; I kept my circle small and never ventured far: the local supermarket, the butcher's and home, that was it. I couldn't risk going further afield and bumping into them.

Sometimes when I'd been lying awake at night in my single bed in St Jude's, twisting and turning and watching the light invade around the edges of the curtains, I would let myself play out a fantasy in my head where I was out somewhere – it was always somewhere picturesque like the shoreline at Donabate beach. The sun would be warm against my skin and the sky would be bright cerulean blue, criss-crossed with vapour trails and the soaring arc of gulls. The Martello tower would be in the background and the marram grass-covered dunes providing shelter to the families sitting on picnic blankets. In the distance I would spot two boys splashing in the shallow water. I would watch them play awhile and then, as I got closer, I would realise it was them – my boys. I'd start running towards them. At first, they'd be confused – sometimes in these fantasies they were even a tiny bit scared – but after a few seconds, they would recognise me too and their faces would change to pure joy. In the dream I would chastise myself for ever thinking that we wouldn't know each other. We'd all run towards one another, splashing through the water, and when I eventually reached them, I would engulf them in huge, smothering hugs as the waves crashed around us over and over again. I would tell them that I loved them and that I was so, so sorry and they would tell me that it was okay, they had forgiven me. That they understood. I had romanticised various scenarios of the grand reunion over the years but realistically I knew that they probably didn't even remember me, let alone know what I looked like. And even if they did, why would they want to reunite with the woman who had tried to kill them?

'They're better off without me. I gave up my right to be a wife and mother that day. Anyway, they'd be fourteen and twelve now, they wouldn't remember me.'

'But you were low, you were desperate. There is a lot more compassion and understanding for people with mental health difficulties nowadays. It might not be too late to repair your relationship with them,' Lucy pleaded.

'What mother contemplates killing her own children?'

Lucy looked at the floor. She had no answer for that. She was clearly disgusted by me and rightly so.

'That's why you have to listen to me, Lucy,' I implored. 'I know what I'm talking about. What I wouldn't give to be able to go back to when my two were small. I'd do it all differently. Don't be like me, I'm begging you. I know what you're going through is different but something like this can get in on you and suddenly you can't see a way out. Everything seems hopeless and then you're not thinking rationally any more. I lost my children because of it but you have the chance to do right by Anabel; please promise me that you won't take Neil back.'

Lucy's eyes were wide as she digested the warning that I was giving her. I was living proof of what could happen when you tried to hide from your problems; they grew, and they shifted, and they magnified until one day they had metamorphosised into a tsunami that washed you away.

31

After hearing Eileen's story, Lucy felt ashamed. Ashamed of how quick she had been to judge Eileen as a weird, reclusive neighbour, a sad, pitiful little woman. Eileen had sunk to the lowest ebbs imaginable and yet she had managed to pick herself up again from the depths of despair. What was overwhelming for Lucy to comprehend was that she had put her own pain aside to come to her aid when she'd needed her.

In opening up to Lucy, Eileen had exposed her soul, parts of herself that she had long ago buried, and Lucy knew that couldn't have been easy, but she had done it because she needed Lucy to understand what could happen if she decided to take Neil back. It was a wake-up call. Lucy realised that if she let Neil continue to do this to her, that she could be the one in Eileen's shoes, all out of hope, despairing and bleak until ending it all seemed like the only way out. Eileen's story had highlighted to her just how fragile mental health could be.

Looking at the spritely, no-nonsense woman sitting beside her in her living room, she couldn't imagine Eileen ever being vulnerable or in such a dark place. Although their situations were different and Eileen's husband hadn't been violent, he had been emotionally absent and had failed to get her the help she so desperately needed. If he had been supportive, she might not have fallen so low, and her life could have been so different. His inaction had destroyed her. Eileen had paid the ultimate price, but what was most heart-breaking was that she didn't want to forgive herself. She had built the walls of a self-imposed purgatory and she was holding herself prisoner inside. It made Lucy determined to help her; she needed Eileen to see that it was time to forgive herself. Eileen had helped her and now it was Lucy's turn to return the favour.

Lucy lifted her phone and went to google Eileen to see if she could learn anything more about her past but then she realised that she didn't even know her surname. It was possible that Eileen had told her at some stage, but Lucy knew she had probably been too preoccupied with her own life to bother remembering it. How ironic it was that Eileen knew Lucy's most intimate secrets and now she knew Eileen's too, and yet she didn't even know the woman's full name, she thought.

Lucy put the phone down on the sofa beside her in frustration. Surely there must be something she could do to help. Eileen had lost her children because the supports weren't in place to deal with her postnatal depression. She had been badly let down. For all she knew, Eileen's children might even be looking for her too and didn't know how to find her. Although Eileen had been adamant that she didn't want to dredge up the past, Lucy really thought she deserved some closure.

Lucy's parents returned downstairs a short time later. Lucy had forgotten she had promised Anabel that she would read her a story after they had given her a bath.

'Sorry, I never came up to do her story.'

'Don't worry, love,' Pete said. 'She was out like a light.'

'Well, I think I'll go up and tuck her in anyway.' Lucy stood up from the sofa. Even though Anabel was already asleep, she wanted to give her daughter the biggest, tightest hug. Eileen's story had hit home with her just how fortunate she was to still be here, to still be able to squeeze her child. Eileen hadn't been so lucky. She had lost everything. Tears pushed into her eyes as she recalled what Eileen had told her

'What's wrong, love?' Noleen asked, noticing the water pooling in her eyes. 'You're looking a bit shook; are you feeling all right? It's not something to do with Neil, is it?'

Lucy shook her head. Where would she even begin?

32

The following day, Lucy had a visit from the Gardaí. They had called to her in the hospital too and were trying to convince her to press charges against Neil, but she was adamant that she didn't want to drag him through the courts. Her parents were worried this was a sign that she was thinking about taking him back. After everything that Eileen had told her, she knew she could never do that, but she was worried that by pressing charges Neil would be sent to jail. She knew Neil ought to be punished for what he had done but she felt so conflicted. The idea of him sitting behind bars in a cold cell horrified her. How could she do that to him? Neil was her husband; he was Anabel's father and she still cared for him despite everything.

The thought of Anabel being led through prison security and sitting opposite her father in a visitation room full of other inmates terrified her.

'On the night of the attack, we had a chat with Ms Murphy next door,' Garda McCabe was saying. Lucy's parents had told her that Garda McCabe had been at the scene on Christmas night, but Lucy had been lying unconscious on the floor at that stage. 'Ms Murphy informed us that there had been another incident previously?'

Lucy felt a fizz of excitement: *Eileen Murphy* – that was her name. Lucy repeated it again in her head to make sure that she wouldn't forget it.

'Lucy,' the Garda was saying, forcing her to concentrate, 'is that correct? Did Neil assault you on a previous occasion?'

She nodded slowly. There was no point trying to deny it any longer. The truth was out there now. As Garda McCabe took a moment to write down the details of the injuries she had sustained that night, she keyed 'Eileen Murphy' into the search engine on her phone. She checked through the results: there were obituaries and some academic by the same name had published a lot of scientific research, but nothing seemed relevant to her neighbour. She tried 'Eileen Murphy Lake' in case there had been any newspaper coverage of the incident at the time but, again, nothing seemed to come up. Next, she tried 'Eileen Murphy Carlingford' – that was the village Eileen had mentioned they had lived in. Once again, Lucy was greeted with a barrage of results but nothing that seemed relevant to the Eileen that she knew. Lucy wanted to help her so badly; although Eileen claimed she didn't want to track down her family, Lucy thought she deserved a second chance – just maybe her family would find it in their hearts to forgive her and she could have the happy reunion that she deserved. She put her phone down again; if Google wasn't going to help her, she was going to have to find another way.

'Lucy?' Garda McCabe was saying.

'Sorry, yes...' she said, bringing her attention back to the Garda.

'I was saying that we strongly advise all victims of domestic violence to press charges. I know it's not easy, but we have trained Gardaí available to support you through the process. We need to send a message to perpetrators that they will be punished. Silence allows these people to thrive.' Garda McCabe tilted her head to the side and Lucy knew that the woman pitied her. She probably saw women in Lucy's situation every day of the week, too scared or unwilling to press charges out of fear, loyalty, or love. She imagined it must be frustrating for her to watch victims forgive their abusers and allow them back into the family home only for the abuse to continue. Eileen's story had frightened her, and she didn't want that for herself. She couldn't take a gamble on her life by believing him when he promised he would never do it again. If she took Neil back and he lost control again, he could kill her and she didn't want Anabel to grow up without a mother. Even if he didn't manage to kill her, the hopelessness of the situation could lead her to do something she had never imagined she was capable of. Either option wasn't nice.

'I'll be in touch to keep you updated on whether the DPP decides to bring their own charges but if you change your mind, you have my number.'

Lucy nodded. Garda McCabe's words had the desired impact, and the guilt overcame her. She knew she had a moral obligation to do something – not just for her sake but for all victims of domestic violence, some of whom were no longer alive to tell their stories, but there were also many more who might never find their voice to speak out. She was still here and, despite everything, she was one of the lucky ones.

'I'll think about it,' she agreed.

33

The sky was slate grey as Lucy stepped outside the house. January drizzle fell softly on her face as she made her way down the driveway. She wanted to call over to Eileen to see how she was doing after her visit the day before. She knew that by confiding in her, Eileen had lifted the lid on a lot of old feelings that she had hidden away and Lucy needed to make sure she was okay. Lucy rapped the knocker against the white PVC door of number 26 and waited.

'Lucy?' Eileen said as soon as she answered the door. 'I must say I wasn't expecting you. Come in.'

'I can go if it's not a good time?'

'No, no, it's as good a time as any. Is Anabel not with you?'

'She's in the house with my mum.'

Eileen nodded but she seemed disappointed.

Lucy followed her inside the house. Although the layout of both houses was the same, it was like time had stood still in Eileen's living room. It was a small, poky room like theirs had been when they had first bought the house. Eileen hadn't broken through the wall to make a large open-plan room stretching the whole length of the house like they had. A brown carpet covered the floor, and the walls were painted plaster pink. A well-worn sofa and armchair took up nearly the whole room. There were various pieces of mismatched furniture that looked as though they had been recycled from a charity shop. Net curtains covered the windows and Lucy reckoned they must have been there since the seventies, but despite the dated appearance of the furnishings, she noticed that Eileen kept everything clean and tidy. Lucy sat down on the sofa and sunk into the valley of the cushion. The fabric was shiny along the armrests from all the people who had sat in it over the years. Lucy reckoned the sofa was older than she was, judging by the state of it. Dora hopped up beside her and curled herself into a ball. Eileen didn't seem to mind the dog being on the furniture.

'I just wanted to see how you were?' Lucy began.

'I'm okay.' Eileen paused. 'Thank you, Lucy... It's been a long time since anyone apart from the medical professionals have asked me how I am.' She seemed touched.

'I know it can't have been easy for you yesterday, going back over all that old hurt, but I want you to know that I appreciate it. What you said to me. You helped me to see how easily it could happen. I'm sorry Eileen, I was too quick to judge you. I think we're more alike than I realised.'

Eileen nodded. 'You remind me so much of myself when I was younger. That's why I had to tell you everything, but you're strong, Lucy, I can see that; you'll survive this. Don't let Neil take away anything else from you or, before you know it, you won't even recognise the person you've become. Trust me.'

Lucy nodded. 'I won't take him back.'

'Well, I'm glad to hear that.'

They both fell quiet and the sound of the ticking clock on the mantlepiece punctuated the air. 'Will I get you a cup of tea?' Eileen offered after a beat. 'You're probably a coffee person but I don't drink it, so I don't keep any in the house.'

'Tea would be lovely, thanks.'

Lucy sat alone while Eileen went out to the

kitchen to make the tea. Dora was snoring gently beside her. She looked around at the walls; there were no pictures or photographs, nothing to tell her about Eileen or the woman she once was. It didn't feel like a home. Lucy supposed Eileen probably wanted it that way.

Eileen returned a few minutes later clutching two steaming mugs. She handed one to Lucy and she took it carefully.

'I searched your name on Google,' Lucy confessed as she sipped her tea. She wasn't sure whether she should tell her or not but since she hadn't discovered anything, she reckoned she was safe enough.

'Me?' Eileen's eyes darkened. 'Why would you do that?'

'I was trying to see if I could help you find out where your sons are now. I'm sorry, I know it's none of my business,' she added sheepishly.

'You're right, it isn't,' Eileen snapped.

'I didn't find anything. Murphy is a common surname.'

'Murphy is my maiden name, so you were wasting your time.'

Lucy hung her head, feeling ashamed. 'I see.'

'Lucy, it's in the past, love. I know you're only

trying to help but I'm okay, honestly. You don't need to fix me. I've made peace with it all. Just leave it now, all right?' Eileen warned.

Lucy nodded. 'Of course... I'm sorry, Eileen. I didn't mean to upset you.' Lucy stood up and placed the mug down on the coffee table. 'I should probably go.'

* * *

'What's wrong?' Noleen asked as soon as Lucy came in the door. 'Did something happen?'

Lucy had filled her mother in on Eileen's story after she had gone home the day before and she had been just as shocked as Lucy was. She said Eileen had been badly let down by her family and society.

'I told Eileen that I had googled her,' Lucy admitted, 'and she wasn't very happy. I feel terrible after everything she did for me.'

'You googled her?' Noleen was shocked. 'What did you do that for?'

'I just wanted to see if I could find out where her sons are now.'

'And did you find anything?'

Lucy shook her head. 'Nothing. There were loads

of hits for her name. She told me that Eileen Murphy is her maiden name, so nothing would have come up anyway.'

'Do you know her married name?'

'No, and I doubt she'll tell me now that I've told her I googled her,' Lucy sighed.

'Oh, Lucy, I don't think you should be getting involved in any of that stuff. Eileen clearly doesn't want to be reunited with them. Leave her alone now and stop digging. Come on, you've enough of your own problems.' She put her arm around her shoulder.

Lucy nodded. 'You're right,' she agreed. 'I was only trying to help but I think I've upset her.'

What had she been thinking trying to meddle in Eileen's business? Eileen had been nothing but nice and helpful to her and this was how she had repaid her. She possibly owed her life to the woman. Would Neil have stopped battering her if Eileen hadn't called the emergency services? Would he have kept pummelling her until she never woke up again? She shuddered to think what might have happened if Eileen hadn't intervened. Remorse for what she had done pricked her. This wasn't a game. Eileen and her family were real people with real feelings. She couldn't try to reunite them like an episode of *Long Lost Family* – life wasn't a TV show. But despite everything, Lucy couldn't shake the nagging feeling that she had to do something – she owed it to Eileen to help her make peace with her past. She was sure that if she could just find out where Eileen's family were now, she could lay some of Eileen's ghosts to rest.

34

Damn Lucy to hell anyway. She just wouldn't let it rest. I was pacing around the kitchen and Dora was following at my heels over and back across the tiles. She was clearly unsettled by my behaviour. I had been doing so well until Lucy started poking her nose into my business. How could she be so insensitive after everything I had told her? I knew she thought she was helping but she would never understand just how painful that chapter of my life was. Ever since I had told her my story, I felt as though I had exposed my Achilles heel to the world, and I hated feeling so vulnerable. I wanted to stay in my bubble where I focused on getting through every day and tried not to think beyond that, because the idea of facing the entirety of the future alone, knowing my family were out there somewhere, was terrifying. I was relieved that she didn't know my married name. From the first day I had come out of St Jude's I had used my maiden name of *Murphy*; Eileen Prendergast was gone now. That woman had been a wife and mother and I was neither. I guessed she would have a hard time finding the boys without knowing their surname, but what if she took it upon herself to go to Carlingford and ask a few of the locals if they remembered me? I'm sure everyone still remembered crazy Eileen who had abandoned her children at the side of a lake while she tried to kill herself. Or maybe I was only flattering myself; perhaps they had all forgotten about me long ago. All I knew was that it would be easy enough to find them if Lucy kept on digging.

I longed to be back in the safety of St Jude's again where I didn't have to worry about any of this stuff. After Lucy had gone home, I thought about picking up the phone and asking Tim to take me back there. Or I could just arrive at the door. They wouldn't turn me away, they'd have to let me in, but then I thought about Dora; they probably wouldn't allow her to come with me. I couldn't abandon her. And then there was Tim too. I'd never be able to look at the disappointment on his face. The thing was, I didn't want to let him down and I knew that he'd feel that he had failed me if I went back to St Jude's. I decided to call him just to sound it all out with him. Dora jumped up onto the chair and was looking at me with her ears pricked. She could sense something was wrong with me.

Tim answered on the second ring. 'Eileen, is everything okay?' He knew I only ever rang him with good reason.

'No, Tim.' My voice wavered on tears. 'It's not.'

'What's happened, Eileen? You're doing so well.' He sounded worried and I knew this would upset him. Sometimes I felt that he was more invested in my recovery than I was.

'I was thinking about the kids...' My voice trembled. 'I'm sorry, Tim, I know you're busy, I just didn't know who else to call.' Unable to hold back the tears any longer, I began to cry.

Dora hopped down from the chair, came over and brushed against my legs as if reminding me that in a world where I had lost everything, she was still here for me.

'You're all right, Eileen, that's my job. I'll be over shortly.'

* * *

Just over an hour later there was a knock on the door. I knew it was Tim. Dora ran down the hall, her stubby tail wagging. As I opened the door to let him in, she immediately ran to him as if relieved he had come.

'I'm sorry,' I said, feeling ashamed as he followed me into the living room. 'I know you've better things to be doing.'

'Don't apologise, Eileen. We all have bad days. I'm glad you called me. So, what happened?' he asked, setting his backpack down on the floor and sitting in the same armchair that he always sat in.

I explained everything to him. I told him about bumping into Ruth McKeever in the supermarket and how unsettled I had been since. Then I filled him in on what had happened next door. I explained about how I'd thought they had the perfect life until little Anabel had knocked on my door that night. I told him about the second assault and how Lucy had been left for dead. I explained to him how I had ended up minding Anabel while Lucy had been brought off in an ambulance.

'It's okay,' he soothed. 'I wish you'd told me about what was happening next door. That was a lot for you to take on; even those with good mental health would struggle being put into a situation like that. Were the Gardaí aware of your history?'

I shook my head. 'I don't think so. I never mentioned it to them anyway. They just wanted a witness statement from me.'

'And the lady next door...?'

'Lucy.'

'How did you end up telling Lucy your story?'

'I wanted to help her. I was worried that she might take her husband back like she had the first time and I wanted her to use my past as a warning, but I hadn't expected her to start digging around! I thought that by telling her my story she would see that she couldn't stay in her marriage. She could end up going loopy like me; that's if he didn't kill her first. I never expected it to bring up all the old pain though... I'm frightened, Tim. The reason I've been able to get through each day is because I've shut all of that stuff away inside my brain. I haven't forgotten about it – I never will – but I try to block it out. But now it's like someone has pulled the end of a ball of wool and it's started to unravel. I'm worried that I won't be able to keep it all in check and go back to the way I was. I can just about get myself through each day as it is but if I open that door back to my old life, I'm not sure I'll survive it.'

'Do you know something, Eileen? I'm proud of you. I know it can't have been easy for you opening up

to your neighbour like that, but you did it and all because you wanted to help her. You might not realise it,
but you've made huge progress by being able to talk
about it to someone else.'

'It doesn't feel that way. I haven't felt this unsettled
since those first few days when I moved in here. Lucy
seems to think she owes it to me to track down the
boys, but I told her I don't want to know about them.'

'Well, playing devil's advocate here, maybe she's
right. Maybe now is the time to make contact with
them again? I've been saying this to you for a while:
it's time to forgive yourself.'

'And what if they don't want to know me?'

'Then nothing changes. You'll be no worse off
than you are now and at least you'll know, instead of
wishing and wondering what might be. You've punished yourself for long enough, you deserve a second
chance. I know I've said it to you before, but I can find
out some details for you if you want?' he suggested.

'No, Tim, I'm not ready.'

'I would support you through it, Eileen.'

I shook my head. 'If they didn't want to know me,
I'd never survive the rejection. It could send me over
the edge.'

'You're stronger than you think, Eileen. Yes, there
is a risk that they won't want to make contact with you

– I acknowledge that there are no guarantees in any of this but there is also a chance that they would. One of your sons would be a teenager now and the other boy isn't far off; teenagers are often curious about their past. They might actually want to see you.'

'They probably don't even remember me,' I spat. Trust Tim to put a positive spin on it all. He seemed to look at everything through rose-tinted glasses. Couldn't the man ever just see things as they really were? Not everybody got their happy ever after; I was living proof of that. 'Anyway, they would have made contact by now if they wanted to get in touch with me.'

'They probably don't know where you are,' Tim said.

'Well, it wouldn't be that hard to find me if they really wanted to.' That gave me a thought, maybe they had – maybe they had tried already. Tim would know. 'Did they ever contact you?' I asked, trying to disguise the desperate hope in my voice.

Tim shook his head and lowered his gaze. 'Unfortunately not. You know I'd tell you if they had.'

Disappointment burned through every cell in my body. How stupid I was for thinking that they might have. 'Well, that tells you everything you need to know then,' I retorted.

'In my experience, these things are tricky. There is a lot of pain for everyone and lots of healing to be done on both sides, but sometimes we have to be brave and take the risk. Why don't we try and open some dialogue with your husband first and see how it goes?'

I shook my head. 'No, Tim, I don't think so.'

'Come on, Eileen, just give it a try,' he coaxed.

'I can't.'

Tim exhaled heavily. This wasn't the first time we had had this conversation. 'Well, if you change your mind, you know I'll help you, Eileen.'

'Thanks, Tim.'

'I'd better head on, I've another visit to do shortly but call me if you get upset again. I'm always at the end of the phone. Day or night, don't ever be afraid to call me.'

I nodded.

I felt better after he had left. He always knew how to calm me down. I lifted Dora up and held her close to me. I looked into her soulful eyes and smiled at her. She responded by wagging her little tail. 'Don't you be worrying about me, silly old girl. You're my family now.'

35

Lucy couldn't sleep. She was lying in bed that night with Eileen's distraught face haunting her every time she tried to drift off. The pain of Lucy's betrayal had been unmistakeable in Eileen's eyes. She loathed herself for what she had done. But even though Eileen had warned her not to interfere, it was as if she hadn't been able to help herself. She needed to make things right again, but how?

Lucy was certain that if she could just give Eileen some information about her family, then once she had calmed down, she would be grateful and forgive Lucy for going against her wishes. It was obvious that the pain of losing her family was a scar that cut deeply; Eileen's pain was a vein that was still bleeding out, but Lucy really believed that if she could know more about her family, and maybe down the line, perhaps even be reunited with them, it would go a long way towards her healing. After everything Eileen had been through, she was scared to look back; she refused to make amends with the past and allow herself to be happy again. She was her own judge, jury and executioner but Lucy wanted to convince her that she deserved to forgive herself. It seemed so unfair – she was still suffering and paying the ultimate price because nobody had reached out to help her when she was sinking. Yes, Lucy knew what Eileen had done was serious and she was lucky no one had died or been seriously injured, but she hadn't been well. There was a risk that her family might want nothing to do with her but what if the boys were out there searching for their mother too or wondering what had happened to her? Something within Lucy told her to keep going. She was sure that this was the best way to help Eileen, even if she couldn't see it herself yet.

Lucy's biggest problem was that, without knowing Eileen's married name, she couldn't really get far in her search. She had briefly thought about driving to Carlingford; she could call into the shops there or maybe visit the parish priest to see if anybody remembered Eileen, but then she had thought about her husband Dan and the boys. What if they still lived there? Lucy knew it was a small village, the kind of place where everyone knew one another. She didn't want to cause these people any more pain by re-opening old wounds. It was too sensitive a matter to just waltz into the village and start asking questions.

Lucy reached out a hand and placed it on Anabel's chest. Sometimes Anabel's breathing was so shallow that she wondered if she had stopped altogether but then she would feel her tiny ribcage rise and fall beneath her palm. Anabel had been sleeping in her bed since she had come home from hospital because Pete was staying in Anabel's room. It was reassuring to have her father in the house with her. Lucy had always felt safe inside her own home but now every sound or creak in the house made her nervous. Neil was still sending her messages and although she knew he was full of remorse, she was worried that in a moment of madness or fit of pique he would break the barring order that had been put in place and try to return to the house. Lucy had to continually re-mind herself that her dad was there, that the doors were locked, that she had the phone number for the Gardaí on speed dial.

And it wasn't just the violence that had been an

issue; it was only now after having some space away from him that she realised how controlling Neil had been. Her mother used to say that she was so lucky to have a man who cooked dinner for her every night, but now Lucy realised it was because he wanted to choose what they ate. If they were watching TV, he sat with the remote in his hand. He decided where they went on holidays. He was in charge of their money too; when they had been saving for the house, he had decided when they could spend money on something or whether they should forgo it. She had also lost touch with her friends. Neil didn't like her going for nights out on her own with them and so, gradually, after she had made up one too many excuses and missed several nights out, her friendships had cooled. They were all little things, things so subtle that she hadn't even noticed that there was anything wrong, but now she could see that the power in their relationship wasn't balanced.

She had had to phone Jenna and explain why she couldn't go to work. As she confessed everything, her friend had been shocked and upset; she had never suspected anything was wrong. Lucy now realised how insipid domestic violence could be; she had been a victim of Neil's control and abuse for a long time without even realising it herself. Lucy told Jenna that she hoped to be able to return to work as soon as she had healed from her injuries. Her parents had said they would help her out financially until she got back on her feet again but now, as she faced life as a single mother, and tried to hold on to their home, she would need every penny she could get.

She knew she was safe now, but she still found it hard to relax. Would the fear ever leave her? She could see how the loss of confidence in yourself could play tricks on your mind and change you as a person forever more. It made her wonder what the old Eileen had been like; had she once been a vibrant young woman with hopes and dreams, unrecognisable from the woman she was now? If anything ever separated her from Anabel, she didn't think she'd survive. She couldn't imagine the pain Eileen felt after all those years spent apart from her children. It made Lucy all the more determined to help her.

Suddenly, it occurred to her that she could try googling all their names together to see if that would bring up anything. She lifted her phone from the bedside table and keyed 'Dan Liam Eoin Carlingford' into Google to see what that came up with. She clicked through the first few results, but it was hard to know if any of it was relevant. She changed the spelling of 'Eoin' to 'Eoghan', the other variant of the Irish name, to see if that brought up anything and this time she was greeted with several French websites. She clicked on to the first one and from her limited school French, it seemed to be a match report. She saw the names *Dan and Eoghan Prendergast* listed below the team photograph. She came out of that website and on to another link to a website for a guest house called La Maison Lavande. The home page had an image of a stylish black-and-white portrait of a family standing in front of an old French farmhouse. The man had his arm draped over the shoulder of a slender woman in a strapless sundress and three boys stood in front of them dressed casually in linen shirts and shorts. The family was barefoot as they stood on the lawn with the sun beating down on them. The house was cut from old stone and timber shutters framed every window. Rolling hills planted with leafy vines stretched out in the background beyond the farmhouse. Thankfully, the website was in English; she scrolled down to read through the text beneath the photo.

Dan Prendergast and French born Sylvie Toussaint met in Ireland but decided to return to Sylvie's home country to follow their dream of restoring an old French farmhouse. The family packed up their life in

Carlingford, Co. Louth and relocated to rural France. Tucked away on a dusty road in Provence, La Maison Lavande offers guests a warm, family run home from home to share the pleasures of French family life. Our family look forward to welcoming you. Dan, Sylvie, Liam, Eoghan and Bastien.

Lucy scrolled back up and looked again at these people, but it was the eyes of the middle boy that pulled her in; his colouring was quite fair. He was freckly with ginger hair and a sunburst of freckles covered his cheeks; he had a pointed chin, and his eyes had the same almond shape as Eileen's. Could it be? Could these people be Eileen's family? Lucy stared at the image on the screen. Could this smiling man with the salt and pepper hair be the same person who had failed to get Eileen the help she desperately needed? Were the handsome, sun-kissed boys the same toddlers that Eileen had abandoned at the water's edge all those years ago? The only thing throwing it though was this woman Sylvie. Who was she? And Eileen had only had two sons, but there was a third boy in the photo. It said that Sylvie and Dan had met in Ireland, so they had definitely lived there at some point. Was Sylvie the mother of these boys, in which case Lucy had the wrong family, or was there a connection to Eileen? Lucy knew it was a stretch; she didn't know Eileen's family name and this Prendergast family now lived in France, but it seemed a big coincidence that they had the same first names as Eileen's family and were also from Carlingford. Although she couldn't be sure, something, a gut instinct, told Lucy that she was on the right track.

36

The next day I heard a knock on the front door. I answered it and saw that it was Lucy again. My heart sank. I knew by her urgency, the way she practically propelled herself into the house, that there was something up with her. *She'd better not come here to start bringing up the past again*, I thought.

'Do you want a cuppa?' I asked. The puffy bruising on her face had subsided a lot and day by day she was starting to look like her old self again, but her arm would be in a cast for a few more weeks so it would be a while before she could go back to work.

She shook her head. 'No, no, I'm fine. I just wanted to ask you something.'

'Well, come in and sit down.'

I sat in the armchair, and she sat beside Dora curled up in her spot on the sofa.

'Eileen?' she began tentatively. There was something about her demeanour; she seemed nervous or fidgety.

'Yes?'

'Now, I know you asked me not to start digging around trying to find your family but—'

I held up a hand to her. 'Lucy, just stop right there,' I warned. 'I told you to leave it alone,' I chastised her, and rightly so. How could I make her understand that she had to stay out of this?

'I know you did and I'm sorry,' she rushed on, 'but I just had to do it, Eileen.' She paused. 'Anyway, I wanted to let you know that I've found something...'

I'll admit that got my attention. I swallowed down a lump that was balling in my throat.

'Well, you see,' she continued, eager to get the words out before I cut her off again. 'I found this family in France... Their surname is Prendergast,' she explained.

My head whipped up and she knew from my face that she had struck upon something. *But France?* She must have the wrong people. 'France?' I mumbled. 'I don't think so...'

'Am I right?' she said. 'Is their surname Prendergast?'

I nodded slowly to confirm. 'It is but they wouldn't
be in France.' I shook my head.

'The family that I found are living in Provence.
They run a guest house called La Maison Lavande. I
can show you a photo.' She fished her phone out of
her pocket and offered it to me.

I didn't take it from her; instead, I shook my head.
'I don't think it's the same family, Lucy.'

'They run it with a lady called Sylvie Toussaint.'

My breathing stalled and the blood seemed to
leave my body. Immediately, my heart began racing.
'S-Sylvie? Are you sure, Lucy?' I could hear a quiver in
my voice.

'Are you okay, Eileen?' she asked, but she sounded
far away from me.

'Sylvie was Dan's work colleague,' I whispered
after a moment. 'She's the lady I was telling you about
that was in the house when I came back from Cork,
when I thought I was going mad...' Tears filled my
eyes, and a huge wave of anger upended me. 'The bastard! The lying, cheating bastard,' I repeated. 'And
she's not much better.'

I knew Lucy was shocked by my uncharacteristic
outburst, but this was a huge kick after all these years.

If Lucy was correct in what she had found, it seemed as though Dan had shacked up with Sylvie and they had moved to France to raise my sons together.

'Perhaps they only got together afterwards,' she suggested, trying to give Dan the benefit of the doubt.

I shook my head vehemently. Although it was possible that Dan and Sylvie had only become romantically involved after I was in hospital, it seemed unlikely. 'I knew there was something going on between them, but my head was such a mess and Dan kept telling me that I was mad, so I didn't trust myself. I should have known.' I was fuming. All those months I had spent thinking I was going crazy, that I was imagining it, when all along my instincts were probably right. I realised then that I needed to know for sure if it was them. I couldn't stay in this limbo state any longer. 'Can I see the photo?' I asked.

She took her phone out of her pocket again, keyed in the website address for La Maison Lavande and handed it to me. Tears streamed down my face as I looked at the black-and-white editorial images of the beautiful family standing outside their stone house with its painted shutters. I recognised Liam and Eoghan immediately. Of course I did, how had I ever thought that I wouldn't? But there was a younger boy with them that I didn't know. The cruellest part was that they looked like the perfect family, and I was the outsider.

'That's them,' I sobbed, tracing my finger over their faces on the screen. 'My goodness, what handsome boys they've grown into.'

'I'm sorry, Eileen. I wasn't sure if I had done the right thing. What a blow this must be to have all your suspicions confirmed.'

'They look happy, don't they?' I smiled through the tears. 'That's all I want for them – to be happy.'

'I think it's time for you to get your family back.'

'How do you mean?' I handed her back the phone.

'You need to travel to France to find them.'

I hiked my brows and looked at her as if she was crazy. 'No way! I can't go to France.'

'Come on, Eileen, you can't let him get away with everything! He gaslighted you.'

'What the hell does that mean?'

'It's a term used when someone does something to make another person believe they are going mad. It comes from a play when a man dimmed the lights in the house, but he insisted to his wife that the lights were not dimming and made his wife believe she couldn't trust her own perceptions; he slowly manipulated her until she thought she was going mad.'

'Well, even so, I'm not going to France. The boys probably wouldn't have a clue who I was.'

'I'd go with you.'

'You?' I couldn't keep the shock from my voice.

'Yes, I could help you. I'm so angry at how you were treated and feel you deserve a second chance with them. Please, Eileen, I can organise it all. You wouldn't have to do a thing.'

'I can't just turn up and knock on their door after all these years!'

'We could contact them first to say we were coming?'

'That's an even worse idea,' I retorted, shaking my head. 'There's no way they'd agree to let me come.'

'So, we'd have to surprise them then.'

I shook my head. 'I'm not going anywhere, and besides, I couldn't leave Dora. Sorry.'

'You can take dogs on the plane. She'd probably have to travel in the hold but it's only a short flight.'

'Absolutely not! I couldn't put poor Dora through that. She'd be terrified.'

'Well, I could ask my mum to mind her,' Lucy suggested.

I shook my head. 'No way. I wouldn't leave her with anyone else. She'd think I'd abandoned her!'

Lucy groaned in frustration. 'Sounds to me as

though you're using Dora as an excuse,' she challenged.

I narrowed my eyes at her. 'And what would you know?'

Lucy knew she had caused enough trouble. She might think me a stubborn old mare but nothing she said was going to persuade me. She stood up to leave. 'I'm sorry, Eileen, I should probably go now.'

I nodded and saw her out to the door. She stepped outside on to the driveway, stopped, and turned back to face me.

'If you change your mind—' she tried one last time.

'I won't,' I said, cutting her off quickly before slamming the door shut after her.

37

Lucy returned next door and found the house empty. Her mother had left a note to say that she had taken Anabel to the shop for a walk and would be back soon. She flopped down onto the sofa and sighed. The situation with Eileen was beyond frustrating. Lucy had finally managed to track down her family, but Eileen was so infuriatingly stubborn that she still wouldn't get in touch with them. Lucy wanted to shake her and make her see that it was time to make peace with the past, but it was like Eileen wanted to prolong her suffering.

Just then she heard the doorbell go. For a moment she thought it might be Eileen; perhaps the woman had had a change of heart or was even a bit curious about it all. She picked herself up off the sofa and went out to answer it. Through the glass side panel, she saw there were two people on her doorstep. She peered out and realised it was Neil standing there alongside Pamela. Lucy felt her blood come to a standstill as if her heart had stopped pumping. Her body felt like those stretchy-men toys that Anabel sometimes got in party bags; her legs were like rubber and she thought they might fold under her at any minute. The bell rang again. She reached up and began fumbling with the security chain. Once she had it secured in place, she opened the door to them.

'You... you... shouldn't be here,' she stammered through the gap.

'Please, Lucy,' Pamela begged. 'We're not here to cause trouble. We just want to talk to you.'

'Go... go before I call the Gardaí.'

'Please don't do that,' Neil said. 'I promise you nothing is going to happen.'

'I have a barring order.'

'We just want five minutes to talk,' Pamela pleaded.

'This isn't fair. You're breaking the law by being here!'

'I'm sorry for doing this,' Neil tried, 'but it's the only way you'll see me. You won't reply to my calls or messages. I'm desperate...'

'Please, Lucy, he's distraught,' Pamela continued. 'I promise you, you're safe. Just hear him out; he has some things he needs to say. Give him five minutes. I'll stay right here with you both.'

She looked at Neil head on. He was pale and he had lost weight. He had lost condition too. He didn't seem as large, and his muscles weren't as defined as they usually were. She saw there was no menace in his eyes, just pure desperation.

Lucy removed the chain and opened the door. 'Come in,' she sighed, beckoning them towards the living area. 'But I'm warning you, my mum will be back soon and if she sees you here, she'll call the Gardaí.'

'Five minutes is all we want,' Pamela said.

They made their way through to the kitchen and Lucy sat in the armchair at the end of the room while Neil and Pamela took the sofa. She flinched as she re-membered the last time they had sat across from one another in this room. Her world had tipped upside down and become unrecognisable since then.

'How's Anabel?' he asked.

'She's doing okay, all things considered.'

He nodded. 'I hate myself for what I've done. I miss you both so much,' he choked. 'Thanks for letting me come in... I wanted to explain everything.'

'Neil, no matter what you say, it's not going to change anything.'

He nodded. 'I just wanted to tell you why I think this happened...' His eyes darted across to Pamela and she nodded at him to continue. 'I've been using steroids,' he admitted. 'I think that's the reason I became violent.'

Lucy was shocked. 'Why would you do that?' she asked in disbelief. She was aware that illegal steroid use happened in the fitness industry, but she thought Neil knew better. Was he really that desperate to look good that he would resort to taking illegal drugs?

'You see all these young guys coming in, bigger than me, more ripped and can lift more metal and I just got sucked into it. I'm so sorry.'

'Where would you even get them? They're illegal.'

'There's a guy that comes into the gym, he gets them. I don't ask where. I think this was why I was losing my temper so easily and turning violent.'

'Are you still taking them?'

He shook his head. 'God no. They've ruined my

life. I've stopped now. I just wanted you to know that it wasn't the real me. When I say I've changed, I really have.'

'Why couldn't you have told me this weeks ago? You could have taken action and it never would have gone this far.'

'I'm sorry, Lu.' His breathing was ragged. 'I'm going to regret it every day for the rest of my life. I hate myself for what I've done to you. I've lost every-thing. My family. My home. And now word has got out that I'm a wife beater and I've lost over half of my customers overnight. If it doesn't pick up soon, I'm going to lose the gym.'

'Am I supposed to feel sorry for you?' she barked.

He shook his head. 'Of course not, but I wanted you to know that I've found a new counsellor; she's much better than the last one. She's already helped me so much. She's given me loads of techniques on how to calm down when I feel myself get angry.'

'He's working really hard, Lucy, I promise you,' Pamela backed him up.

'I'm glad you're getting help but I wish you'd done it earlier. We might not be in this mess if you had.'

'It's not his fault, love. His father was a brute.' Pamela shook her head as she recalled the horrors they had experienced. 'He witnessed things that no child should ever see.'

'I know you and Neil had a tough time of it at the hands of his father but that's not an excuse for what he did to me.'

Neil sat there with a hangdog expression on his face. He was like a child before her, allowing his mother to do the talking for him. It was pitiful.

'Neil's dad never once showed any remorse for his actions. Neil is devastated, Lucy. I've never seen him so low; he's not eating, he's not sleeping. I know what my son did was completely unacceptable but maybe in time you'll see how hard he's trying and how much he's changed...' Pamela suggested.

Lucy shook her head and looked directly at her husband. 'Even before you were violent, Neil, you've always been controlling. You isolated me from my friends and made all the big decisions in the house. It's only since I've been away from you that I can see how bad it was.'

'His life is ruined,' Pamela pleaded. 'He's being punished enough. He's Anabel's dad and he was a good husband to you before all of this happened.'

Neil shared a look with his mother and Lucy knew there was something else that they wanted to say.

'What do you want from me?' she asked eventually, growing tired of it all.

'Well, I wanted to ask you not to press charges, Lucy...' Pamela began tentatively. 'I know the Gardaí might decide to bring their own charges but without a statement from you then it's less likely to make it to court. Please, Lucy, I'm begging you, he's learnt his lesson; he's getting the help he needs. Don't send him to jail.'

Lucy felt the lid lifting on her rage. She was angry with Neil for what he had done, not just to her but to Anabel. His actions had torn apart their family unit but now hearing their words, she realised that this visit was for selfish reasons. The reason Neil and Pamela were here was for damage limitation.

'It's all about you, isn't it? You're calling here to clear your conscience; you don't respect me or the fact that by calling here unannounced you've distressed me and broken the law. It's all about what *you've* lost, how *you're* suffering. You nearly killed me, Neil! Our daughter is traumatised and probably will carry that with her for the rest of her life. Our marriage is over; I've lost my husband. I've lost my trust in the man I thought I would spend the rest of my life with. I've wasted enough time on you.' Lucy stood up, indicating that she wanted them to leave.

Neil turned and pleaded with her. 'Please, Lucy, I'm begging you. I know you might never forgive me for what I've done but please don't send me to jail. I won't survive in a place like that.'

Lucy turned to Pamela. 'Get him out of here this minute before I call the Guards.'

38

Two days later I answered a knock on the door to find Lucy standing there clutching a small bunch of daffodils.

'A peace offering,' she said, smiling nervously at me as she handed me the flowers. 'I owe you an apology. I'm so sorry for interfering and causing you upset.'

I took them from her and brought them up to my nose to smell. Daffodils have always been my favourite flower; their spiky yellow heads were a bright pop of sunshine after a long winter. It had been years since anyone had ever bought me flowers. Immediately, I felt my anger soften towards her. I had been feeling guilty for how we had left things.

'Come on in,' I invited.

She followed me into the living room.

'So how are you?' I asked. I stood clutching the flowers. I didn't even own a vase to put them in. I'd have to use a glass or something.

'You'll never guess what happened after I went home the other day.'

'Go on,' I urged.

'Neil and his mother called around.'

'Are you serious?' I sat down in my armchair, still holding the daffodils, and Lucy took a seat beside Dora on the sofa. 'How did I not see them? I see everyone who comes and goes from your house.' I had been upset after Lucy had gone home that day and somehow I must have missed it. 'I hope you called the Gardaí?'

Lucy shook her head. 'He said he wanted to talk,' she admitted.

I couldn't believe what I was hearing. 'Oh no, Lucy, please don't tell me you let him in?'

She nodded. 'I know, but don't worry, it was fine. Neil admitted that he had been taking steroids and he thinks this is the reason why he got so aggressive.'

'Is that his excuse?' I spat. 'Lucy, love, promise me you won't take him back.'

'Don't worry, Eileen, that's not going to happen. I

thought he had come round to apologise but then he and his mother showed their true colours when she asked me not to press charges!'

'The sneaky bastard; he's only out for himself. You know you could report them; they shouldn't have set foot near your house, let alone tried to influence your decision to press charges. That's another example of him trying to have control.'

'You're right,' Lucy sighed. 'I can see that now. I feel like I've been walking around blindfolded all this time. How did I not see this before?'

'Don't be beating yourself up. Controlling be-haviour can be very subtle. The main thing is that you finally see him for what he is.'

'So, how've you been doing?' she asked. I could see from the way her face was pinched in concern that she was genuinely remorseful.

'I'm okay.'

'Well, I'm truly sorry for interfering.'

'Look, it's done now,' I sighed. 'Do you want a cuppa?'

'I'm okay thanks, Eileen. I know it's none of my business,' she continued. 'It's just that I feel so furious about it all and it's not even my life.' Her face became worked up as she spoke. 'I just don't know how you're not angry.'

'Of course I'm angry!' I retorted. 'Since you told me about them all living in France like one big happy family, I can't help but wonder what might have been,' I admitted. I'd had a lot of time to think; normally, if I thought about that chapter of my life, I'd close the book sharply and push the thoughts from my head as soon as they entered, but since Lucy had called over two days ago, I had forced myself to dwell on it. I had allowed my head to go to places, to trawl through old memories that I usually wouldn't let myself think about. I had lifted the lid on the ache that I had long suppressed and, through digging around in the depths of my darkness, had pulled out the most painful of memories. I had allowed myself to feel it all – grief, pain, anger and despair, instead of trying to avoid it like I usually did. I felt sad for the younger me and couldn't help but wonder if perhaps it was the stress of the situation between Dan and Sylvie that had been the trigger for the avalanche that followed. One domino falling into another that had set off a chain reaction of events that led me to the place I was now in. It was too late for regrets, the past had happened and me feeling sorry for myself wouldn't change anything, yet I couldn't help but wonder, *what if?* Could I have avoided being hospitalised if things had been different? Would I still be living with my family, raising my sons, watching them grow from boys to men and preparing them to go out into the world to live their lives?

'They stole so much from you; they robbed you of everything – your whole life has been shattered by what they did,' Lucy said heatedly.

'I can't blame everything on them. I was the one that went into the lake; no one was pushing me in.' I paused. 'But I can't help but look back on it all now and wonder if maybe I wasn't as crazy as I thought? Maybe I had good reason to be suspicious about Dan and Sylvie. I might not have sunk so low if I hadn't had to deal with my worries about them having an affair on top of everything else. Maybe that was the thing that tipped me over the edge?'

Lucy nodded. 'It can't have helped, especially if you were already in a bad place. These things can spiral and before you know it, they've got out of hand and there is no going back. You know I can finally see that we have more in common than I ever thought. When Neil hit me the first time, he twisted it around so that it was my fault. That I had provoked him by asking to have a second baby. I blamed myself. If I hadn't started on about it, he wouldn't have hit me. It took me a while to realise that although that might have triggered his anger that time, even if

I had never brought up the subject of a second baby, there would have been something else. It's the same for you. We were both manipulated when we were vulnerable.'

I nodded sadly at her. 'I went to the library yesterday and looked them up,' I confessed. 'I saw all the photos and read about their guest house. They really are living the dream,' I said wryly.

'You know you can take Dora on the ferry?' Lucy said tentatively as if she could read my thoughts.

'What are you saying, Lucy?'

She was smiling nervously at me. 'I mean, if Dora is the only thing stopping you,' she continued, 'she can go with you to France; you are allowed to bring dogs on the boat.'

Since I had learnt about Dan and Sylvie, fuelled by anger and so much sadness for what might have been if I had just opened my eyes, I had been wondering if Lucy's suggestion of taking a trip to France wasn't as hare-brained a notion as I had first thought. I had so many questions that I wanted to ask. I wondered if the boys remembered me? Was Lucy right, could they be curious teenagers searching for me too? The last thing I wanted to do was distress the boys, but as for Dan and Sylvie, they were fair game. I couldn't give a damn if I upset them or upended their perfect life. 'You're actually serious about this, aren't you?' I asked her.

'I looked up the rules,' she went on eagerly, 'so she needs to be microchipped and have a passport and then get a rabies shot. I know it sounds like a lot, but the vet can do it all for you.'

'Well, anyway,' I continued. 'Whatever about Dora not having a passport; I don't have one either.'

'I could help you get one,' she suggested.

'And what about Anabel? Who will mind her while you're off gallivanting around France?'

'She can come with us. She'll be off school for two weeks at Easter; we could go then. She'd love a road trip with you and Dora. I should have my cast off and be back driving by that stage and it will give you enough time to get your passport sorted out.'

She made it all sound so easy. Could I do what she was suggesting? Hearing that Dan and Sylvie were together had changed me. I now felt wronged, and maybe Dan needed to hear a few home truths, but then I would think about the boys; they looked so happy in their set-up now, the last thing I wanted was to cause them any more pain.

'Maybe,' I sighed. 'We'll see.'

Lucy's face broke into a huge grin, and I knew she

felt that this was huge progress. 'So, you'll think about it?'

I nodded. 'I said *maybe*. I'm not promising anything. And I'll need to check with Tim...'

She punched the air in victory, and I couldn't help but crack a smile at her. 'Lucy Walsh,' I said, wagging my finger at her. 'I rue the day you ever came into my life.'

39

My heart ratcheted as the car emerged from the bowels of the ferry and the roads spread out like arteries in every direction. They were different to the roads at home; everything was wider, bigger, faster. I looked across to the driver's seat at Lucy as she pulled her sunglasses down from her hair and placed them over her eyes, indicated and merged with the traffic. Her cast was gone, and her face had healed. She was as glamorous as ever with her perfectly applied make-up and her blow-dried hair tumbling over her shoulders. It was good to see her getting back to herself again. She seemed totally unfazed by driving on the wrong side of the road and the journey we were about to take. Lucy had bought a harness for Dora to keep her safe in the car and she was strapped into the back seat alongside Anabel. Anabel was delighted with her travelling companion and kept pointing out the window, showing things to the little terrier.

We had a twelve-hour drive ahead of us as we travelled over five hundred miles south through the French countryside towards the village of Lourmarin which was close to where La Maison Lavande was located. Lucy had shown me pictures of the village on her phone; it looked so pretty, nestled at the foot of the Luberon mountains with sandy-yellow buildings, winding cobbled lanes and cafés fronting on to shaded squares.

We had boarded the ferry in Dublin Port and sailed overnight to Cherbourg which had taken over eighteen hours. Lucy and Anabel had slept for most of the crossing, even Dora had snoozed all night, but I hadn't slept a wink in the narrow cabin bunk as my mind churned through everything that lay ahead of me on the other side of this journey.

'Are you sure about this?' I asked Lucy for the hundredth time since I had sat in her car. I longed to ask her to pull over and turn back. How had I let her talk me into this? I had been having second thoughts about it all since we'd left St Brigid's Road the day before. Just over twelve months ago I had been a resident in St Jude's; if someone had told me then that a year later I'd be heading off on a road trip through rural France, I never would have believed it. I would have said they needed to be put into St Jude's with me. The whole thing seemed preposterous even to me. What had I been thinking agreeing to come here on a wild goose chase? What on earth was I going to say to Dan after all this time? To the boys? How could I explain it all?

'Yes!' she replied unequivocally without taking her eyes from the road. 'I've told you a million times that you deserve to find out what happened to your children. There's no going back now.' She was young and fearless and seemed blissfully unaware of how much was at stake here. She saw this as some kind of empowering girls' trip – 'You're taking back the reins of your life,' she had called across to me from her bunk in the cabin last night, but I was feeling terrified and not remotely empowered. Lucy wanted to fix me and lay the ghosts that haunted me to rest; I just hoped it wouldn't be a wasted trip.

I had called Tim and told him that I was considering going to France to try and find the boys. I had expected him to talk me down and tell me it was a crazy idea. Then I would use that as an excuse to Lucy not to go. *Sorry, Lucy, Tim doesn't think it would be a good idea...* But Tim had had the opposite reaction. He had actually encouraged me and even offered to help with the organisation of the trip or any paperwork that I might need. I was starting to think I was the only sane one amongst them.

Anabel and Lucy were singing along to a Taylor Swift album that Lucy was playing. It just left myself and Dora looking around the car in bewilderment, wondering how the hell we had got here.

We stopped to get petrol in a large motorway service station on the outskirts of Paris. While Lucy queued with Anabel to get food, I thought about running away. I could hide in a toilet, I reasoned, then try and hitch a lift back to Cherbourg, but instead I dutifully returned to the car.

Lucy had helped me with the application for my passport; she had brought me to the Garda station to get it witnessed and signed. She had kept the pressure on me, sorting and organising everything until I couldn't back out. She had also brought me and Dora to the vet to get her travel paperwork in order and her rabies jab. Although I would have welcomed some complications – that would have been a perfect excuse not to travel – it had been remarkably straightforward. Lucy had booked the ferry and then a *chambre d'hôtes* in Auxerre for one night to break up the journey. She had booked an Airbnb in Lourmarin and she had asked me how long I wanted to stay for. But I hadn't a clue – I might be sent packing after an hour, or if things went better, then maybe we'd last a little longer. I had also been worried about the cost of the trip; I didn't have much money left over after I got my social welfare every week, but Lucy had insisted that she wanted to cover it all, that it was her way of thanking me, so she had gone ahead and booked the Airbnb for three nights and said we could leave earlier if things didn't work out as we hoped or extend the stay if it was going well.

We had gone around in circles discussing whether or not we should make contact with Dan first and tell him we were coming. Arriving unannounced felt underhand somehow, like I was throwing a sneaky blow or trying to catch them on the hop. I hated the idea of arriving into their lives like a grenade – a grenade that they'd thought had been defused a long time ago – but I also knew Dan might refuse to see me if I gave him a heads-up. A visit from Dan's mentally unstable ex-wife and mother of his two sons could scupper the perfect life he and Sylvie had created for themselves in France. So, in the end, we agreed that I didn't have much of a choice and we were just going to arrive on their doorstep.

The only thing left was to convince myself that I could do this. That I deserved to do it, but it was the thought of seeing my boys that drove me on whenever I felt doubtful. I hoped they would at least be receptive to me; I didn't care about Dan, but I knew my heart might never recover if my sons rejected me. I swallowed a huge lump in my throat. That was the fear in all of this: what if they wanted nothing to do with me? I felt so vulnerable, so exposed. For years I had hidden away in St Jude's, keeping myself to myself, but now I had no walls to hide behind. I was laying my feelings bare for them and they could trample all over me if they so wished. We were on the road; we were coming.

40

We arrived in Lourmarin the following afternoon. Although it was April, the sun was beating down and people sat outside cafés and bars under the shade of awnings. We checked into our apartment and Lucy asked if I wanted to head straight to La Maison Lavande. I shook my head. I was tired and grubby from all the travelling, I wanted to compose myself and look presentable, so we agreed to wait until the next morning. We were so close – I was just mere minutes away from seeing my two sons after a lifetime apart – but I didn't want to rush it. I had waited this long; I could do another night. I knew it had to be done properly. It was important that I make a good impression after all this time. The last time Dan had seen me I had been a mess; if I was going to have any chance at reuniting with my family, I knew I would need to show him that I had changed.

We decided to go for a stroll around the village instead. We found a café in Place de l'Ormeau and ordered some food. Nobody batted an eyelid when Dora trotted in beside us. I realised that French people loved their dogs. They went everywhere with their owners: petrol stations, restaurants and shops. Dora was having a great time, making new acquaintances and sniffing other dogs that lay at their owners' feet in the cafés. I was starting to see the attraction of the laid-back French lifestyle. Here in Lourmarin, everything seemed to go at a slower, more relaxed pace; people strolled to the fresh market and stocked up on fruit and vegetables. I imagined them taking their time over the stove at home as they perfected rich dishes.

I saw every hour on the clock that night as I lay awake in a strange bed thinking about what was going to happen the following day. When I got up the next morning, my stomach was somersaulting. Lucy suggested we go for breakfast first, but I shook my head; I knew I'd never be able to eat anything. It felt as though I was waiting on the executioner to fire his gun.

'Let's just get this over with,' I sighed.

While I showered, she went to the boulangerie down the street and returned with coffee and croissants for her and Anabel. I laid my clothes out on the bed: one pair of jeans, a pair of black trousers and one grey and one black T-shirt. I asked Lucy what she thought I should wear. I wanted to look presentable; it felt important to me that Dan see me looking well. I didn't want him judging me. She had suggested the jeans and then had told me to try on a sage-green blouse belonging to her.

'I can't wear that,' I spluttered. 'It would never fit.'

'Of course it will; you're only a tiny thing. It'll be fab on you.'

I took it reluctantly and when I had buttoned it up, I stood and looked in the mirror. To my surprise I found that it actually fit me and, what was more, Lucy was right, it suited me. I had brought the only pair of shoes I owned, a sensible black leather pair with flat rubber soles. They weren't the most stylish, but they were practical and, let's face it, I didn't have much need for dressing up in my everyday life. When Lucy saw me putting them on, she suggested I try on her low suede ankle boots instead. When I looked in the mirror, the whole outfit worked. She had offered to do my make-up for me as well. She said make-up was like her armour; it gave her confidence. I needed all the confidence I could get, so even though it had been years since I had put any of that stuff on my face, I agreed to let her do some wizardry on me.

'No fancy stuff,' I warned her.

'I promise I'll keep it natural.'

I barely recognised my reflection as I stood before the mirror. The make-up gave my skin a glow, it softened my wrinkles and evened out my tone. Having ditched the black clothes and my sensible shoes that I normally wore, I looked years younger. Lucy was beaming at me, and I knew she was delighted with how it had turned out.

'Wow,' Anabel said. 'You look so pretty, Eileen.' She turned back to her mother. 'Mammy, when are we going to see Eileen's family?' Lucy had explained to Anabel in the simplest terms our reason for travelling to France. She understood we were here to see my family, but she didn't know any of the history or drama.

'Soon, love. We're going to drive over there shortly, but Eileen is going to go into the house on her own,' Lucy explained.

'I want to come in too.' She pouted.

'I know, love, but it's important that Eileen goes alone first. We'll wait outside in the car.'

'But that's not fair, I want to see them,' she complained.

'I need someone to mind Dora,' I said. 'And you're the only other person she will stay with.'

'Okay then, I'll do it,' Anabel agreed readily.

Lucy winked at me. I clipped Dora on to her lead, and we set off downstairs to where the car was parked. Bright slices of blue morning sky were visible between the shaded narrow streets as we walked along the cobbles to the car park.

'Right then, are we ready?' she asked when we reached her car.

'As ready as I'll ever be,' I groaned. Although I longed to put this off, a part of me was excited. I was so close to seeing my sons again after all this time; they were within touching distance. Nervous anticipation bubbled up inside me.

If I did see them today, how would it go? Would we tearfully run towards one another with open arms like I had imagined us doing or would it be more reserved, taking everyone a little longer to warm up? Or would I even get that far? Dan could turn me away at the door, crushing all the hopes and the anticipation that had built as I prepared myself for this moment. I pushed the thought from my brain. I had come this far; right now I couldn't face any other alternative. I was going to see my boys today.

41

As the car bumped along the winding road, I studied Lucy's phone intently, following the blue line on the directions that Google Maps was giving me.

'Turn right here,' I said.

'Here?' Lucy asked, jamming on the brakes. 'Are you sure, Eileen?' She eyed the road warily. 'It's practically a dirt track.'

'Well, that's what it says.' I pointed at her phone. It had taken me a while to get used to following the navigation and several times I had given Lucy instructions either too early or too late, causing her to miss the turn.

From the driver's seat Lucy glanced at the phone in my hand, then she signalled right and we turned down the narrow road, sending clouds of dust flying up on either side of the car.

'They didn't exaggerate when they said it was remote,' she muttered after we had been driving along the track for several minutes.

'What if we have the wrong house?' Eileen asked.

'We have their postcode. It's definitely where they live.'

'But what if they're not home?' I asked. Doubts were multiplying faster than fruit flies inside my head.

'Well, then we'll just have to come back again this evening.'

'Or they might have gone away somewhere on holidays or something.' I had purposely chosen to come on a Saturday in the hope that the boys would be off school but what if they had headed off somewhere for the weekend?

'Look, Eileen, try to relax. I know you're nervous but we've come this far. You deserve this.'

I thought about Dan and Sylvie shacked up together with my boys and that gave me the resolve I needed to do this. It was the seething anger that burned within me even after all these years that spurred me on.

The morning sunlight spread a carpet of white

across the landscape. In the distance I spotted a hilltop village with biscuit-coloured buildings clinging perilously close to the edge. Below it, a field of leafy vines stretched down the valley as far as the eye could see. Being here, witnessing the vibrancy of the colours, the different sights and scents, was a feast to my senses. For all those years, I had lived a life hidden away behind the drab walls of St Jude's, and now it was like I had awoken and someone had switched on the colour in my world again.

Eventually, we saw a turn-off with a sign for La Maison Lavande and my stomach lurched. 'Here we go,' I sighed as Lucy turned the nose of the car through a set of large pillars. The tyres crunched along the gravel as we followed a winding avenue lined with elegant cypress trees on each side. Soon a beautiful stone farmhouse with blue painted shutters came into view. I immediately recognised it from the website, but seeing it now in all its full colour glory, I could admire it properly and it was beautiful. I saw what had persuaded Dan and Sylvie to pack up everything to move over here. A grove of gnarled and stooped olive trees provided shade at one side of the house. There were a couple of flat-roofed outbuildings with a creeper covering the walls and in front of them there was a Peugeot car parked further up ahead in the driveway. Someone was at home. I didn't know if I should be relieved or terrified. A part of me would have been glad of the excuse to turn around and go back to Lourmarin.

Lucy had the sense to park the car a distance back from the house. She silenced the engine and let down the windows and immediately Dora stuck her head out and sniffed the air which was infused with scents of lavender, rosemary and thyme. We could hear refrains of children's laughter coming from behind a hedge in the distance. We listened for a moment to boyish squeals and roars followed by the sound of splashing water. Were they my boys? I realised they must be playing in a pool behind the hedge. My heart soared.

'Are you okay?' Lucy asked.

I swallowed down the fear that was balled in my throat and placed my hand on the door to open it. I was excited, I was terrified; so many conflicting emotions were tumbling around inside me. Dora hopped out first, then I climbed out and set my feet on the ground. It felt strange walking in Lucy's heels over the lumpy gravel. She and Anabel got out too and we followed the voices over to the pool.

We found a gap in the hedge which allowed us to view them without being noticed. The three boys that

I had seen on the website were playing in the pool. I was mesmerised.

'That's them, isn't it?' Lucy whispered, standing alongside me as we watched through a gap in the hedge.

I nodded, too overcome to speak.

'Are you okay?' she asked again.

Tears filled my eyes at the sight. They were beautiful. Long-limbed and lean, rangy like teenage boys that are growing faster than you can feed them. They were both sun-kissed, even Eoghan who was always the fairer of the two; his bright red hair had now turned a rich auburn shade and his once pale skin was lightly tanned. He resembled me, he always had since the day he was born. Droplets of water arced through the air and glistened like crystals on their hair as their played; their carefree shrieks carried on the gentle breeze.

I looked around the garden but didn't see any sign of Dan and Sylvie. They were probably inside the house. The three boys were speaking rapid French to one another and throwing a ball around. Suddenly, Liam swam to the side and used his arms to hoist himself out of the water. He ran along the pool edge, drew his legs up to his chest, wrapped his arms around them, then he cannonballed into the water.

He was so close I could feel the water splash my face. The other two boys were laughing. I couldn't help but smile at them play. How carefree they seemed, how happy.

Anabel was tugging on Lucy's arm. 'Who are those boys?' she demanded.

Lucy put a finger to her lips, warning her to lower her voice. 'They're Eileen's family,' she explained in a whisper. We were just metres away and she didn't want them to become aware that we were watching them through the hedge.

'Can I go play with them in the pool?' she begged, ignoring her mother's request to be quiet.

'No, sweetie, we have to let Eileen do this on her own.'

I handed the lead to Lucy, walked along the hedge until I found a large enough gap to pass through and took a step forward. I couldn't help myself. I had planned on knocking on the door and talking to Dan first, explaining everything and why I was here in the hope that I could convince him to let me see our sons, but now it was like I was magnetised by them. I heard Dora give a little whine after me, followed by a yelp. I knew she wouldn't like me leaving her but I had to do this. I made my way across the lawn until I reached the scorched terracotta tiles surrounding the pool.

They didn't notice me standing there at first, they were too wrapped up in their play.

I was just metres from them, my own sons. I never would have imagined as I had held them both in my arms as tiny babies that one day we would have been separated like this – that I would have done something so terrible to cause us to be torn apart from one another. How I loved them; it felt more powerful than ever, a physical force being expelled from me. The love hadn't faded; it felt stronger now, pent-up and ready to explode from deep inside me. I wanted to jump into the water and take them into my arms. I longed to pull them from the pool, bundle them into Lucy's car and drive far away from here but I knew I had to tread carefully. I didn't want to scare them in any way. Now that they were within touching distance, I couldn't bear to lose them all over again.

Suddenly, the youngest boy pointed at me and shouted something in French at the others and they all turned around and looked at me. Liam jumped out of the pool. *'Maman!'* I heard him cry, and my heart picked up speed. He remembered me. Of course he did. He was running towards me and I opened my arms to embrace him, waiting to feel his force collide against me. How I had longed for this moment. I had let myself imagine and play it out in my head for so long and now it had finally arrived. I was about to be reunited with my son but I was left standing there with my arms outstretched as he ran past me, his eyes wild with fear as he hurried into the house. 'Maman! Maman, viens!'

Who was he calling Maman, I wondered. Surely not Sylvie?

'It's okay.' I put my hands up to assure Eoghan and the younger boy that I meant no harm but they looked terrified of me. 'I won't hurt you. I promise.' I took a step closer to them but they both backed away to the corner of the pool furthest from me. It was only then that I realised that they had no idea who I was. Moments later, Liam came back out of the house followed by Sylvie running behind him. She was wearing a faded blue T-shirt, cut-off denim shorts and a pair of flip-flops. Her dark curly hair was piled up on top of her head. As she stood on the patio I watched her face change through expressions of shock to disbelief before settling on fear when she recognised me. I had come face to face with the woman who had stolen my life.

42

Sylvie was looking at me warily as she waited for the boys to get out of the pool. Did she really think I would hurt them?

'*Garçons, rentrez à l'intérieur!*' She spoke in a panicked tone.

'I don't want to cause you any trouble, Sylvie,' I said, walking towards her with my hands up, but this seemed to frighten her even more. Her face was seized with terror as she gathered them close to her.

She began backing away from me and her tone became more frantic. '*Vite, vite!*'

'*Maman, c'est qui, cette femme?*' the youngest boy was crying.

'*Vous m'avez entendu? Je vous ai dit de rentrer à l'in-*

térieur. Maintenant!' Sylvie shouted as she ushered the boys inside the house.

My two sons ran past me without so much as a second glance. There was no glint of recognition in their eyes; in fact, they were purposely avoiding looking at me. They were scared of me – they were scared of their own mother. I wanted to say, 'Liam, Eoghan, it's me – it's Mum,' but I realised with disappointment that felt as though it was pulverising my bones that I was a complete stranger to them.

As they hurried into the house, I stood at the side of the pool wondering what I should do now. Should I follow Sylvie inside and demand to talk to my sons? Dan and Sylvie had stolen years of my life from me. They had got away with it for long enough; was it time to reclaim what was mine or had I caused enough trouble simply by arriving unannounced? Suddenly, I began to doubt myself. Perhaps I had done this all wrong. I had terrified the boys and that had never been my intention. I was confirming what Sylvie and Dan believed – that I was mad. And now the boys thought so too. I should have made contact with Dan first, explained to him that I was coming and even if he refused to see me, at least I would have forewarned him without scaring the whole family. This had been a bad idea; how on earth had I let Lucy talk me into this trip? I should have left the past in the past. The whole thing was complete madness. Defeat and despair poured into me like concrete. This had been my one shot at seeing my children and I had blown it. I turned around and began to make my way back to the garden where I had left Lucy and Anabel just a few minutes ago.

'Eileen?' I heard a voice say from behind me.

I turned around and saw Dan standing there. Although his dark hair was now salt and pepper and his stubble was peppered with grey, he looked much the same as when I had last seen him. He had the dark tan of a man who spent a lot of time outdoors. He looked fit and athletic and I had to admit he had aged far better than I had.

His face was pinched in disbelief. 'Is it really you?'

I nodded.

'Wh-what are you doing here?'

'Can I sit down?' I asked, gesturing to the wooden furniture. Suddenly, my legs felt like jelly, the sun felt too hot on my skin and I wasn't sure if I could stand up for much longer.

'Sure,' he said, gesturing to the table and chairs. 'Take a seat.'

I flopped down into the chair and he took the seat opposite me across the table.

'Why are you here, Eileen?'

'I wanted to see the boys.'

'It's been over ten years since we saw you. You can't just turn up out of the blue! You're after giving everyone a fright,' he admonished.

I nodded, knowing he was right. 'But would you have let me come if I'd asked?'

'I don't know...' he admitted. 'So... how have you been?'

'I had a tough few years, but I'm getting there.'

'When did you get out of the hospital?'

'Well, I've been living on my own for the last year. They gave me a house in Crumlin and so far it's been going okay. How have you been? The boys?'

'They're good.'

'So when did you move to France?' I ventured.

'Over ten years ago now. The boys don't even remember living in Ireland.'

'You and Sylvie though...' I said, shaking my head. 'Turns out I wasn't imagining it. I was right about you two all along, wasn't I?' I pushed, feeling braver now. 'So what happened? As soon as you had the crazy wife locked away in the lunatic asylum, you both had a clear run at it?' I goaded. 'And then you took my children and moved country without even telling me!'

His fingers clenched tightly around the timber

arms of his chair. 'That wasn't how it happened.'

'Oh yeah? So it wasn't going on before?'

'I'll admit we had got close before you went into hospital. Things were so difficult at home, I felt so stressed and didn't know who to turn to. I was working hard to keep a roof over all our heads and I never knew what was facing me coming home at the end of every day. You were struggling and I didn't know what to do to help you. Sylvie listened to me; she was the only person who knew what was going on at home. I don't know why but I felt I couldn't tell our friends or families. I didn't want them to judge us. Then when you went into hospital, I was left alone with two young boys, trying to mind them and work at the same time. She helped me through that awful time and was a great support to us. It just kind of happened from there... Sylvie is a good woman, Eileen. She took me and the boys on and loved them like her own.'

'You wiped me out of your life like you would clean a fingerprint smudged on glass. You never even visited me once!'

'I was angry, Eileen! I swear to God if I saw you, I would have drowned you in that lake myself.'

I winced at the vitriol in his words.

'How could you just abandon them there like

that?' he continued. 'Anything could have happened to them! I was angry with you for a long time afterwards. Angry that you had put us in that situation, that you had let things get so bad that you resorted to trying to drown yourself in a lake. I tried so many times to get you to go to see a doctor but you were so stubborn and kept telling me you were fine. I knew you weren't well but I never thought you'd do something like that!'

'Do the boys know who I am?' I pressed.

He shook his head.

I felt my breath snag in my chest. 'Do they remember me?'

He shook his head again.

'You never told them about me?' I asked in disbelief.

'They were only babies when you left, Eileen.'

I cut across him. 'I didn't leave—'

'Well, whatever way you want to say it, they don't remember you. Sylvie has been their mother for nearly their entire lives. She is the only mother they've ever known.'

That stung. It seared and roasted every fibre of my being right down to the marrow of my bones. 'So they don't know that she isn't their real mother?' I cried. My overarching fear had been that they would have memories of being left at the lake that day and watching me being pulled from the water, but never that they would have forgotten all about me. How could I have been wiped clean from their lives? This hurt more than the knowledge that Sylvie had been acting as their mother, the fact that they didn't realise they had another one. Sylvie and Dan had created a perfect life for their family here in Provence but it was all a charade.

'What was I meant to do, Eileen?' Dan blazed. 'Put yourself in my shoes. You abandoned them at the side of a lake where anything could have happened to them, then I was left to take care of two tiny boys on my own and try to hold down a job to keep a roof over our heads, while you were in the hospital. Was I supposed to tell them about you and what you tried to do? You weren't around, remember? I was their only parent, I had to do it all on my own and I made the decision not to tell them about you because I thought it would be easier that way.'

'So you came to France so you could pretend you were one big, happy family?' I quipped.

'We came here for the boys' sake. People were talking in the village. It felt as though they were whispering everywhere we went. If we went to the shop, the checkout lady would tilt her head to the side in pity and make a fuss of the boys. I hated it. I hated the extra attention people gave us. I hated everyone pitying us. I didn't want the boys growing up with that. I didn't want them to get older and learn what had happened from someone else or be taunted in school by another child. Kids can be cruel. I wanted to protect them from all of that and for them to have as normal a life as possible so that's why we decided to move to France for a clean start.'

When I heard it from his point of view, I had to admit I could understand his reasons for moving away. It would have been difficult for the boys growing up in a small village where people never forgot and even years later tongues still wagged.

'I didn't set out to hide the truth from them,' he continued, 'but they were so young that they didn't even remember you, then myself and Sylvie were to-gether and I guess we just naturally became a family. The boys adored her from day one. Sylvie is a bril-liant mother; she took the boys on and loved them like they were her own. We wouldn't have got through that period without her. After we moved here, we had Bastien and you've never seen brothers so close. The boys don't know anything different.'

'Well, it's time for them to know the truth,' I said.

'Please, Eileen,' he begged. 'Don't upset them.

They had enough tragedy in their early years. Don't make them revisit the past. They're happy now. I know this is difficult for you but this is the only family they've ever known. If you go in there, you're going to disrupt their whole world.'

'But you're all living a lie at my expense!' I protested. 'They have a right to know about their mother – their real mother.'

'Sylvie is their mother,' he said.

'She is not their mother,' I hissed through gritted teeth.

'They're happy, Eileen. Isn't that what you want for them? If you love them, you'll go home and leave them alone.'

A buzzing sounded in my brain. I did love them. I loved them endlessly from the tips of their toes right up to the hairs on their heads and even though they didn't know I existed and they believed that Sylvie was their mother, I wanted them to be happy. Was it too late now? I had given up my family on the day I'd decided to end it all. My head started to spin, I wasn't sure what was right or wrong, fair or unfair any more. I had to get out of there.

I nodded at Dan. 'I think I should go now.' I pushed back the chair and stood up.

He stood up too, his face awash with relief. I felt

his eyes on my back as I walked off and headed down the avenue to where Lucy's car was parked. Although it had only been about thirty minutes since I had left her, it seemed like a lifetime ago. Everything had changed since then. It felt as though my heart had been ripped out of me in that time. All the hope and anticipation that had bubbled up inside me when we had driven along the dusty roads had been stripped away, and now I realised that everything was gone. I had nothing left. Nothing to be hopeful for. The dream that maybe one day I would be reunited with my boys had been fuelling me on my darker days back in St Jude's and I had hoped by some crazy serendipity or chance circumstances we would be brought together. I now realised that would never happen because my sons didn't even know that I existed. How could they be looking for something they didn't know they had lost? They would never come knocking on my door, I would never get a surprise letter in the post saying they were searching for me because, as far as they knew, they already had a mother. Sylvie was their mother and I was no one. And was Dan right? If I truly loved them, I would want them to be happy and, if that was with Sylvie, then maybe that was the price I had to pay for what I had done.

43

Lucy and Anabel were bent over, picking wild roses that were growing along the side of the driveway. The flowers smelled so fragrant compared to the ones that grew in her garden at home that always died at the first hint of frost. They were pungent, the aroma cleansing. Anabel was rubbing the petals against her wrist, to make perfume. Suddenly, Dora started pulling on the lead and began yelping. They turned around and saw Eileen coming down the lane towards them. She had only been gone for a short time. Lucy knew it wasn't a good sign if she was back again this fast. Even from a distance she could tell from Eileen's demeanour that it hadn't gone well.

'Eileen!' Anabel cried as she turned around and saw her coming down the lane.

Eileen seemed sunken, like a smaller woman than the woman who had rushed through the hedge to see her boys. Anabel ran towards her.

'Do you want some perfume, Eileen?' She began to rub the rose petals on Eileen's wrist before she could even answer.

Lucy picked herself up from the ground.

'So how did it go?' she asked as Eileen neared her.

'Let's go,' Eileen said, lifting Dora up and cuddling her close.

'Come on, Annie, we'd better go,' Lucy said.

They all climbed into the car and as soon as Anabel had her seat belt on and Dora was fastened into her harness, they set off. It took several manoeuvres but she managed to turn the car in the narrow width of the lane and they headed back along the road towards Lourmarin.

'Did you see your family, Eileen?' Anabel asked from the back seat.

'I did,' she replied.

'Can we come back another day and play with the boys in the swimming pool?' she asked.

'We won't be going back there,' Eileen said, not offering any other information. Lucy longed to ask her what had happened at the house but she could see she wasn't up for talking. Eileen seemed distraught; clearly, it had gone worse than either of them had expected. They all fell quiet until they reached the car park near where they were staying.

Back at the apartment, Lucy put the key in the door and Eileen trudged inside after her.

'I'm going to go lie down for a while,' she said wearily. Dora followed her into the bedroom and Eileen shut the door after them. Guilt smacked Lucy. This was all her fault. She had persuaded her to come and now her grand plan for a reunion for Eileen and her sons had backfired spectacularly.

'What's wrong with Eileen, Mammy?' Anabel asked.

'She's just a bit tired, sweetie. We'll let her sleep and you and me will go out for a walk.'

While Eileen stayed in her room with Dora, Anabel and Lucy took the stairs down to the ground floor. It was just after noon and the spring sun had warmed the cobbles around Lourmarin. People were beginning to sit for lunch at the tables outside the cafés. Lucy stopped in a shop and bought some fresh, crusty bread and cheese, then they headed up to Château de Lourmarin. It was a steep climb and they had to take several rest breaks for Anabel. They walked around the château, admiring the antique Provençal style of the interior, and then they ate a picnic in the gardens.

As she showed Anabel how to make a daisy chain, she thought about Eileen. Lucy was worried about her. It was her fault that they were here; Lucy had pressured her into it when perhaps she was still too fragile to take on such an ordeal. Lucy should have listened when Eileen had tried to tell her that she wasn't ready. Eileen had been right all along, but Lucy had been adamant that travelling to France was the right thing to do. Lucy just hoped this wasn't going to set Eileen's recovery back.

'Can we bring this home for Eileen?' Anabel asked, holding up the daisy chain when they had threaded enough daisies together to make a necklace. 'She looked really sad when we went to see her family.'

'I think she'd love that.'

They stood up, gathered up their belongings and began walking back.

There was no sign of Eileen when they arrived back at the apartment. Lucy knocked gently on her bedroom door but there was no response, so she opened it. She saw that Eileen was awake, lying fully clothed on top of the bed linen just staring at the ceiling. She looked broken. Dora was curled up beside her. It was as if someone had removed her essence since they had gone to La Maison Lavande. She was now a hollowed-out version of herself, a shell of the woman she had been before.

'Do you want to talk about it?' Lucy asked.

She remained silent.

'What happened earlier?' Lucy tried again, but once more she was met with silence. Lucy sat down onto the bed beside her. 'Was it that bad?'

Finally, Eileen spoke. 'It was worse.'

'Tell me about it.'

Eileen lowered her gaze from the ceiling and her eyes met Lucy's. 'The boys don't remember me. Sylvie has raised them as their mother, they don't even know I exist. Coming here was a waste of time.'

'Oh, Eileen!' Lucy gasped, her heart aching for this woman. Just when things seemed to be going in the right direction, life had once again punched her full force in the gut. Lucy had never for a minute considered that this might be the outcome. Yes, she knew that Dan and Sylvie were living together in France but she had assumed she was acting as a stepmother to them, and that they knew their real mother – the mother that they were estranged from – was back in Ireland. Even if they didn't have memories of Eileen,

Lucy had presumed that Dan had told them about her, but no, he had cut her out of the picture. Moving to France really had been a fresh start for them all, Lucy thought grimly. He had wiped the slate clean, wiped the boys' mother from their lives and replaced her with Sylvie.

44

My head was thumping. Bitter disappointment, adrenaline and despair; all of it a toxic combination inside my brain. The voices in my head were back. They were telling me I was crazy. I didn't like this feeling. Unsure of myself and uncertain of everything. Who could I trust? Was Dan giving me friendly advice or was he manipulating me again? Could I trust my judgement or was it impaired? It was exactly how I'd felt back when the boys had been babies and I couldn't trust my own decisions.

'You can't let him away with this!' Lucy was incensed. 'He has stolen enough happiness from you. He is living a lie at your expense; you're paying the price for his perfect life. It's time that the boys know the truth.'

'It's too late now. I don't want to upset them; you saw them, Lucy. Their life looks idyllic. How happy did they look splashing around in that pool? What could I offer them in comparison?'

'They're your flesh and blood. That counts more than any material stuff,' Lucy argued.

'They are living this happy life, blissfully unaware that they once had another mother. I know I wasn't a good one but I tried...' I choked. 'And I loved them so very much.'

Lucy put her arm around me and pulled me close. 'I know you did.'

'I just want to go home,' I said. 'It was a crazy idea coming here.' I wanted to be back at home in St Brigid's Road with Dora. I realised for the first time since I had left St Jude's that St Brigid's Road now felt like home to me. I thought about Tim and how proud he would be when I told him that I felt safe there. I didn't feel safe here; I was too exposed; it was too painful to think of my boys being only a few kilometres up the road and yet there may as well have been several thousand between us.

'You've come this far; you have the right to get to know your sons.'

'I lost all rights that day at the lake.'

Lucy shook her head. 'No you didn't, Eileen, you were ill and you had no support network. You need to stop blaming yourself. It's time Dan told them the truth.'

'I'm tired, Lucy. Can we not just go home?' I begged. I wanted to close my eyes and never wake up again.

'I called the ferry and there is no room on tomorrow's sailing so we have to stay until Monday.'

I sighed and looked at her sceptically. She was probably lying to me too. I didn't know who to believe any more. There seemed to be no end to this torrent of hell.

'Come on, Eileen, can we just try again?' she pleaded. 'This will be the last time. You can't let Dan get away with this; the boys are old enough to know the truth. You deserve this, Eileen. Let this not be a wasted trip. What he's done is wrong – he lied to you and now he's lying to your sons. He's manipulating you all over again, can't you see that?' Lucy implored. 'It has to end now. I know it will be a huge shock but that'll be Dan's problem to deal with the fallout; he's the one who lied to them.'

'He told me that if I loved them, I'd go home and leave them alone.'

'Of course he did! Can't you see that he's gaslighting you all over again? He's pushing the blame back on you, making you believe that *you're* the problem when all along it's been him. You can't trust that man. Please, Eileen, let's go again. I'll go with you this time; I won't let him push you around.'

'But it's going to be the same story, Lucy. He's hardly going to roll out the red carpet and invite me in.'

'Well, we need to give him an ultimatum: either he tells them the truth or we're going to do it for him.'

She made it all sound so easy. That was the thing with Lucy, she had a way of simplifying even the biggest of dilemmas.

'Come on, Eileen,' she urged. 'You've nothing to lose here. You can't let Dan and Sylvie win. Think about all of the years that you missed out on. Think about how things might have turned out if he had been a proper husband to you and had your best interests at heart, instead of manipulating things to suit himself and Sylvie. It worked for him that you were classed as mentally unstable and locked up in a psychiatric ward, it allowed them to go public with their relationship, people probably even pitied Dan. *God love him after being left on his own with two boys.* They probably applauded Sylvie. *Wasn't she so good to take them on*? Your hospitalisation paved the way for their relationship. Liam and Eoghan are still children but Dan and Sylvie won't be able to hide this forever. You're named on their birth certs so when they're old enough, they are going to discover the truth and when that time comes, will they think that you never tried to find them? Dan will probably feed them more lies about how you never wanted them and they might never forgive you for that.'

Lucy had thrown up something I hadn't even considered. If the boys ever saw their birth certs, they would have questions of their own. I didn't want them to think that I had walked away from them and forgotten all about them. I needed them to know that I was looking for them. That I regretted my actions every single day. That I would never stop loving them.

'You have to try now,' Lucy continued. 'So that the boys know the truth and then it's their decision about how to take things forward. Worst-case scenario, the boys refuse to see you and you'll be going home without meeting them and even if that happens, you're still no worse off than you are now.'

'That would finish me off completely.'

'Come on, Eileen. Let's just try it again,' she begged. 'I'll stay with you and I promise if it gets too much, we'll go home and I'll never mention it again.'

'All right,' I agreed. I was already regretting it.

45

We turned on to the dirt road again and this time Lucy didn't question my directions. The sun was starting to set now and the sky was bleeding orange. We parked in the same spot as we had earlier that morning. Lucy silenced the engine and I stepped out of the car. I opened the rear door to let Dora out. Anabel, nearing her bedtime, had dozed off in the back seat beside her. I clipped Dora's collar to her lead then looked at the view down the hillside as the sun lowered over the fields of vines. The dying sun had washed everything pink and the late evening light gave the place an enchanting quality. Crickets clicked and birds trilled sweetly on the evening air. In another life I would have stopped to admire the tranquil beauty of our surroundings, but not that evening. Was I really doing this? It felt like a dream, like I was watching myself from afar.

Lucy rolled down the window a crack for Anabel, then she climbed out and locked the car. We walked up the avenue under the shadows of the cypress trees and when we rounded the bend, we saw them. They were getting into the car. Dan and Sylvie were climbing into the front seats of the Peugeot while the three boys were getting into the back. Were they heading off for a nice family dinner? I wondered. Or maybe they were off to the movies or to watch a concert and now here I was ready to unravel it all.

It was Liam who spotted us first. He was waiting at the side of the car for Eoghan to move over so he could get in too when he suddenly stopped and pointed. '*Regarde, Papa, elle est de retour!*'

Eoghan and the younger boy, who I now knew was called Bastien, immediately jumped back out of the car and turned to look at me. Dan and Sylvie soon followed and the five of them stood on the gravel staring at us.

'*Maman, pourquoi elle est là encore une fois?*' Bastien was asking Sylvie.

I looked across at Lucy, doubting what we were about to do. She reached for my hand and whispered,

'We're doing this, Eileen.' She continued marching forward, dragging me along with her.

Dan started walking forwards, closing down the distance between us. Panic flitted across his eyes. 'We don't want any trouble; please just leave,' he ordered.

'We're not going anywhere,' Lucy spoke up. 'Enough is enough.'

Dan turned to me and nodded towards Lucy. 'Who is she?'

'That's Lucy; she's a friend of mine,' I said, finding my voice. 'She helped me to come here today.'

'Well, I think you both need to go back home now. Nothing good will come from this,' he warned.

Lucy stood defiant. 'We're not going anywhere until you tell everyone here the truth.'

'This isn't the time or the place,' he hissed. 'We're heading out to meet friends. Look, if you want I'll meet you in town tomorrow... We can talk then.'

I glanced at the boys standing in the background with Sylvie; they all looked terrified. The worry on their young faces made me hesitate. Maybe this wasn't the right way to do it. The last thing I wanted to do was frighten them. They were all looking to Sylvie for reassurance. She put her arms around Bastien and Eoghan and pulled them close to her. It was a natural instinct; I knew she was only trying to protect them but it made me wild with jealousy. Lucy looked across at me, her eyes urging me to speak up. She was telling me that the time had come. It was now or never.

I took a deep breath. 'No, Dan,' I said, forcing myself to sound braver than I felt. 'We're doing this now. If you don't tell them the truth then I will.'

Liam stepped forward and made his way towards us. '*Papa, comment connais-tu cette femme?*' he asked as he came up and stood alongside his father.

Dan turned back to Sylvie. '*Rentrez-eux à l'intérieur*, Sylvie,' he shouted.

I turned to Sylvie. 'I don't wish to cause trouble.' Her eyes were as hard as flint as she turned away from me and steered the boys in the direction of the house, but Liam made no move to follow.

'*Mais elle est qui, Papa? Comment te connaît-elle?*' Liam demanded, more urgently this time.

'Liam, *viens!*' Sylvie ordered.

Reluctantly, he began walking into the house.

'Okay, Eileen, let's talk,' Dan said, throwing his hands up in the air once we were alone. 'What the hell do you want?'

'Why don't we start with telling the boys who Eileen really is,' Lucy suggested.

'Why don't you let Eileen speak for herself,' he snarled at Lucy.

'Don't speak to her like that, Dan!' I warned with a steely edge to my tone.

Dan turned back to me then. 'I don't get what you're trying to achieve? You can't just turn up out of the blue after all these years. You're after scaring everyone. You're crazy!'

The phrase felt like a gunshot ringing in my ears. Anger started to fizz through my veins. It was what he always used to say to me. That I was crazy. That I was imagining everything when all along my gut instinct had been right.

'That is the last time you will ever call me that,' I warned through gritted teeth.

He cast his eyes down to the dusty earth.

'I just want my boys to know the truth,' I forced myself to continue.

'They're not *your* boys. You gave up all rights to them when you abandoned them at the side of the lake that day,' he retorted.

'I can't change what I did in the past,' I said, finding a strength I didn't know I had, 'but they need to know the truth, Dan. If you're not going to tell them I'm going to go into the house and do it myself,' I threatened.

His demeanour changed: the anger dissipated into something resembling panic. I knew he was rattled.

'Just think about it, Eileen,' he begged. 'Do you want to shatter their world? Because that's what you'll do if you tell them.' His eyes were pleading with me to stop.

I didn't want to make them unhappy, but what Lucy had said about the boys discovering that Sylvie wasn't their real mother at some point in the future and then thinking that I never tried to find them had really resonated with me. I knew I couldn't take that risk. I nodded. 'It's time, Dan. I'm not leaving here until they know the truth so either you tell them, or I will.'

He brought up his hands and ran them down over his face. Then he exhaled heavily. 'I'll go get them.'

Lucy and I waited while he went into the house. It seemed to take forever.

'Do you think he's coming back out?' I said to Lucy.

'Let's just give him a few more minutes.'

Eventually, he returned with Liam and Eoghan trudging alongside him. They were both looking at me warily; I knew they were confused about what was going on. In their eyes, I was the crazy lady who had turned up on their doorstep and started causing trouble in their perfect world. I hated myself for what I was about to do to them but now, as they stood before me, I had no choice but to keep going. I just hoped that after I explained myself, they might see things from my point of view.

'I think this is better left between all of you.' Lucy squeezed my hand. 'I'll go back to check on Anabel in the car; shout if you need me.'

'*Qu'est-ce qu'il se passe, Papa?*' Liam pleaded with Dan as we all sat down at the table.

I listened as Dan spoke to them in French and, judging from the expressions that fleeted across their young faces, he was telling them the truth. At last. I watched Liam as his jaw dropped to the ground, stunned and disbelieving. Clouds of tears filled Eoghan's eyes and he began shaking his head. '*Non, Papa, non*,' he kept repeating. They both looked distraught by what Dan had just told them and I felt awful that I was the person responsible for causing them this pain.

'Do they understand English?' I asked Dan.

He nodded. 'They're fluent in both languages.'

'Boys,' I began. 'I'm so sorry. I never meant to upset you.'

'Well, then why did you come here?' Liam blazed. I noticed he spoke English with a French accent.

'For a long time I've wanted to get in touch but I was too scared to make contact. Then I thought about you both as adults in the future and how you might discover the truth for yourselves and I didn't want you to think that I never tried to contact you. I wanted you both to know that I'm here if you ever need me.'

'It's too late for that. Dad said you abandoned us at the side of a lake when we were only babies!'

I nodded, relieved that Dan seemed to have spared them the details of my suicide attempt. I had expected this reaction. Why should they forgive me when I couldn't even forgive myself? 'I did, but I wasn't well; my mental state wasn't good. I was very sick back then. I spent a long time in hospital afterwards.' There was no point trying to explain to them that Dan had been unsupportive or that I suspected he'd been having an affair with Sylvie; they were children, they didn't need that level of detail and I knew I ran the risk of losing Liam and Eoghan altogether if I bad-mouthed the parents they so clearly adored. They would obviously side with Dan and Sylvie over this stranger who had come crashing into their world. If I was ever going to have a relationship with them, I would need to tread carefully. It would take time; I would need to build their trust brick by brick.

Liam was shaking his head in disbelief. 'When I was younger, I used to have these horrible nightmares where I was standing by water and I'd be screaming but no sound would come out and I could never get my voice heard no matter how hard I tried or how loud I'd shout. I'd wake up terrified. It got so bad that I was afraid of going to sleep. I never understood why it was always the same dream. Now it makes sense.' Tears swam in his eyes.

It crushed me to think of my son being traumatised by lingering memories but not understanding why these nightmares were tormenting him. 'I'm so sorry, I have so many regrets. I look back on it all and I'm ashamed of what I did. I know I missed my chance to be part of your lives. I realise that. I just wanted you to know the truth and that I love you; I always have and always will. I need you to know that. I was afraid you would grow up and think that I didn't bother to try and find you.'

Eoghan stabbed his finger at me. 'It's too late now. Why did you come here? You are a stranger.' He pointed back towards the house. 'Sylvie is our mother. You can't come here and try to change that!'

'You mean nothing to us,' Liam agreed. 'Get away from here.'

'Look, Eileen, maybe you should go.' Dan stood up. 'This is a lot for them to process and they're upset.'

Water clouded my eyes. I made to leave. 'All I want

is for both of you to be happy.' My voice wavered on tears. 'And I can see that you are very happy here. If you ever need me, I'll always be there for you.'

I turned then and began walking down the driveway, wondering if I would even make it as far as Lucy's car. My legs were as wobbly as a newly born foal's and I felt bone-crushing exhaustion descend upon me. I had accomplished what I had come to do – I had finally met my sons – yet instead of feeling elated, like I had always imagined, I didn't think I'd ever felt so low. For all those hours I had spent staring at the walls in St Jude's visualising what our reunion might be like, it was fair to say, it had never been like this. My sons were angry and I understood that. It was only natural given what they had just learnt. I had felt the truth was important but now that it had been revealed, I wondered if I had made the right decision by coming here or had I selfishly put my own need to be reunited with them ahead of theirs? Was I really so naïve to think that a maternal bond could supersede everything else? I meant nothing to them; how had I ever thought that I might? Too many bloody romantic notions had filled my head and I hadn't even considered that they might not want to see me. Sharing the same blood, carrying them for nine months, meant nothing – a mother was clearly the person who put the graft in, who tended to them when they were sick, who helped with their homework, who tucked them into bed at night and gave them hugs when they were sad. Being flesh and blood counted for nothing if you weren't around to put the work in and raise them. I knew I should be grateful to Sylvie for stepping into my shoes; she had clearly done a good job. Maybe one day I would find it in my heart to be thankful to her for taking on my boys and loving them like her own but I wasn't there yet. Perhaps I should have left it to fate. I should have let them discover the truth themselves and let it be their decision whether they wanted to contact me. I felt as though I had shattered their fragile teenage years and ruined the last days of their childhood.

46

They drove back to Lourmarin in silence. Lucy knew by the way Eileen returned to the car, her shoulders sagging, her head dropped in defeat, her gaze falling to the ground, that it hadn't gone well. Eileen looked smaller somehow, even more diminutive if that was possible. It was as if she had folded in on herself, like a building collapsing during demolition. She seemed to have been broken in the time since Lucy had left her to talk with Dan and the boys. Rather than ask her any more questions, Lucy decided to give her some space and wait until she was ready to talk.

Twilight had descended across the fields of Provence and the mauve sky blended into the landscape. Anabel was still asleep in the back with Dora perched on the seat beside her. When they reached the apartment, she hoisted her sleeping daughter up onto her shoulder and, without saying a word, Eileen helped her to open the doors so she could lift her inside the building. She tucked Anabel up in bed beneath the crisp linen sheets, then she came out to the living area. Lucy found a wine opener in a drawer, then uncorked a bottle of local Luberon wine which had been left as a welcome gift by their Airbnb host. She found two glasses in a cupboard and gave them a rinse under the tap before pouring the wine. She handed a glass to Eileen and even though Lucy knew she didn't usually drink alcohol, she took it gladly. Lucy watched Eileen's eyes water as the wine burned its way down her throat. She guessed Eileen hoped it would block out the pain and obliterate the sadness in her heart.

'What happened?' Lucy asked eventually once Eileen had taken a few sips from the glass. She couldn't stand the silence any longer.

'They don't want to know me,' Eileen admitted, looking crushed.

'I'm sorry, Eileen. That's awful.'

'I spent a lot of time over the years picturing how a reunion might go but I never imagined it like this.'

She shook her head despondently. 'They see Sylvie as their mother and I'm the outsider.'

'Maybe you have to give them time,' Lucy counselled. 'Think of the shock they've had. Put yourself in their shoes – we've arrived here out of the blue and turned their whole world upside down. Everything they believed to be true about their life up to now has been found out as a lie. They're still only children, at the end of the day. They don't have the reasoning skills or the experience that we have to know that life doesn't always work out neatly like a present wrapped with a perfectly tied bow. They're at such a young age; think back to yourself at that age and how black and white things seemed when you were a teenager. They don't yet understand that life isn't always clear-cut and often times there are many more murky grey shades in the middle. When you're young you think your parents are infallible, that they have all the answers, but grown-ups make mistakes too – even the parents they love and adore will make mistakes and that's what Liam and Eoghan need to get their heads around. I think if you give them some space and time to process it, they'll come round. I'm sorry it didn't go like we hoped, but I'm so proud of you for making this journey and taking this step.'

'But that's it; it's all over now. This was my one

shot and I blew it. What if I never hear from them again?' Eileen asked, fear lurking deep within her pupils.

'You've no control over that but you've done the right thing. The truth is out there now and there's nothing else you can do. It's up to them now...'

'That's what I'm afraid of. They might never forgive me...'

'Trust in them, Eileen,' Lucy begged. 'The boys that I saw were two very well-adjusted young men. With a bit of time to process it all they might come round.'

'Do you know something?' Eileen asked, placing the glass down on the coffee table and looking at Lucy head on. 'For someone so young you're very wise. I underestimated you when we first met. Appearances are deceptive because you're one of the kindest, most generous women I've had the good fortune of meeting in my life. I'm still not sure we've done the right thing by coming here but I'm thankful I'm able to call you my friend.'

Lucy felt herself start to blush, caught off guard by the surprise compliment. 'You've helped me too, you know. I might not even be here if it wasn't for you,' she said quietly.

'Sometimes it takes someone else to help us see

our problems clearly,' Eileen continued. 'You could see that I wasn't truly living; I thought I was but you could see I needed to journey on this path to forgiving myself. You saved me, Lucy, when I didn't even realise that I needed saving.'

'And look at everything that you did for me.' Tears filled Lucy's eyes. 'You could see that I needed to leave Neil before I could. If you hadn't stepped in and shared your story with me, I'm not sure I ever would have woken up to what was going on. I kept making excuses for him. I was ever the optimist thinking that that was the last time he would raise his hands to me. That he had learnt his lesson. That he really was going to change this time. One day Anabel might have woken up to find herself without a mother, so thank you, Eileen, for getting through to me. I wouldn't have had the courage to talk to my friends or my mum about it; I was worried that if I confided in them they would always hold it against him like a blot on his copybook and I didn't want that. I guess I wanted to hold on to the perfect image that people had of us – the teenage sweethearts, the young, madly-in-love couple living their happy ever after – it was hard to let go of that. I was afraid they'd judge me or put pressure on me to leave him when I wasn't ready to take that step. I can be stubborn and I know if they had told me what I should do, I would have shut them out and done my own thing. But by sharing your story, it helped me to see it for myself. You made me see that Neil wasn't going to change.'

Lucy hadn't seen Neil since he had turned up on her doorstep with his mother. He was still staying with Pamela and, with the help of their respective solicitors, they were trying to navigate the court system to formally separate. After considerable thought, she had also agreed to press charges against Neil. It was the thought of Anabel falling victim to the same circumstances when she was older that had frightened her into taking action. She needed to be a good role model for her daughter and show her what was, and was not, acceptable in a relationship. She also knew she had a duty to ensure that Neil never did this to any other woman. The road ahead was daunting and her whole chest sometimes seized with anxiety whenever she thought about Neil staring at the four walls of a cell or having to one day bring Anabel to visit him in jail, but Garda McCabe was guiding her through the process and reassuring her with every step that she was doing the right thing.

Lucy never thought she'd be in this situation, facing a marriage breakdown before the age of thirty, but as she had learnt from Eileen's situation, life didn't always work out the way we envisaged. Not everyone got their happy ever after. Anabel was doing well though. Sometimes she woke up during the night crying hysterically after having a bad dream and Lucy would have to take her in her arms and console her, reassuring her that she was safe, but she had never once asked if her daddy was coming home. She had accepted that her father wouldn't be living with them and would instead be staying with Granny Pamela without any questions. Even though she was so young, Lucy felt she understood enough to know that he couldn't live in the house with them. In fact, Anabel almost seemed relieved. Through their solicitors they had agreed that Neil would get access to Anabel only with his mother Pamela present. They would need to get a formal custody arrangement put in place in time, but for now this was what worked. In fairness to Neil, he was so full of remorse that he never disputed anything with Lucy and although they were both different people now, she dearly hoped they could emerge from this experience relatively unscathed and perhaps even amicably, all things considered.

'I never thought I'd be friends with someone like you but I'm so thankful you came into my life,' Lucy said to Eileen. She meant every word. Lucy had emerged from some of her darkest days and although she would always bear the scars, she was rebuilding herself. Eileen had helped her more than she would ever know. Lucy just hoped that the feeling was mutual. She hoped Eileen had no regrets about meeting her and the journey they had undertaken together, not just physically, but emotionally too.

'Eileen, you were so brave to come here. It took courage beyond what you ever thought you had in you to face your past like this but I'm so proud of you. I know the outcome wasn't what we had hoped for but you tried; you tried to reach out to them and no matter what happens they will always know that. I hope that it's given you some peace in your heart.' Although Eileen hadn't got the happy ending she deserved, Lucy prayed she had set her on the path to healing.

'Well, even if they did change their minds and want to get in touch, I didn't give them any details and I doubt Dan will help them to track me down,' she sighed.

'You could write a letter to them, so that they have your address if they ever need it,' Lucy suggested.

Eileen looked at her sceptically. 'They'd probably rip it to pieces and put it in the bin.'

'They might but they might also have the good sense to hold on to it, you know, for the future.'

Eileen nodded, slowly warming to the idea.

Lucy got up from the sofa and began opening the drawers in the kitchenette. She was sure she had seen a notepad with the Airbnb host's contact details somewhere. She found it inside a drawer and smiled when she saw Anabel had used a pen to decorate the paper with misshapen hearts. She located a pen and handed them both to Eileen. 'Here,' Lucy said. Then she fell quiet and let Eileen put her words down on the paper.

47

THREE MONTHS LATER

Lucy pulled into the set-down area in front of the terminal building and I climbed out of the car. She popped the boot, then I lifted out my small suitcase.

I opened the rear door, leaned in and gave Dora a scratch behind her ears. 'Now you be good for Lucy and Annie,' I warned, wagging my finger at her.

'Good luck, Eileen,' Anabel chimed beside her. 'Here, you can have this.' She handed me the cloth comforter that never left her side. It was a square piece of muslin; it looked to have once had a polka-dot pattern but that had long faded.

'I can't take that,' I spluttered, touched by the child's kindness. Lucy had told me that she had slept with it every night since birth and was never seen without it.

'I'll mind Dora and you can mind Dotty.'

I looked at Lucy for permission. 'Go on,' she urged. 'I think this is Anabel's way of wishing you good luck.'

I felt a well of emotion erupt inside me at what a huge gesture this was from the child. 'Well, thank you, love. I'll take good care of it and you promise me you'll take good care of Dora.'

She nodded solemnly.

'And go easy on the treats.' I raised my brows. 'I don't want to get in trouble with the vet about her weight again.'

'I promise I will,' Anabel giggled and I knew as soon as I'd gone inside the terminal she'd be giving the little dog some more.

'Right then,' I exhaled as I hugged Lucy goodbye. I wanted to cling on to her and never let go but I knew I had to do this. 'I'd better go.' I followed the signs for departures and wheeled my case into the terminal building, my heart thumping wildly inside my chest.

I was heading to France to see Liam and Eoghan. After I had written the letter to the boys, I had addressed it to Dan, feeling that it was the right thing to do as they were still only children. I wanted to do everything properly now and it was only fair that I communicate through their father in case he thought I was trying to be underhand by contacting them directly.

I had thought the chances of Liam and Eoghan actually receiving my letter were pretty slim but, as Lucy had said, it was worth a shot. I had been sure Dan would rip it up as soon as he opened the envelope and realised who it was from, but a part of me had hoped he might hold on to it and give it to the boys if they ever asked about me in the future. So nobody was more surprised than me to receive a reply scrawled in teenage handwriting just a few weeks later. It had been written by both boys together and was quite short but polite. They explained how surprised they had been by my visit and that they had asked their father lots of questions since. They seemed curious about me and asked questions about where I lived and what my life was like in Dublin. They had ended it by signing both their names.

I had immediately set about replying to them and brought Dora to the post office to send the letter off that very same day. A couple of weeks later they wrote again and slowly, back and forth through our letters, we got to know one another.

We kept them very general: I told them about my

house, about Dora and what Lucy and Anabel next door were up to and they told me about school, their family and their sport. Liam was a good footballer while Eoghan preferred to play the guitar. Although they often referred to Sylvie as *Maman*, I loved opening their letters and I counted down the days until a new one would arrive. In one letter Liam asked for my phone number and suggested we could call one another instead of writing. It felt like a tiny step forward in our blossoming relationship. Although I had my landline, I still didn't have a mobile phone and I thought this was probably a good time to get one so I asked Lucy to help set me up with one. We went to the supermarket together and she helped me to buy a pay-as-you-go one. I gave Liam my new number and he explained to me how to use Face-Time. Eoghan didn't have his own phone yet so he usually joined in on the call with Liam. It was so much better seeing their faces as we talked. They were both growing into handsome young men. The summer sun had bronzed their skin the colour of caramel since I last saw them at Easter. They would laugh when Dora, ever the attention-seeker, climbed up onto the back of the sofa behind me and photo-bombed the call. On one call Liam asked me why I had called her Dora and I explained how I had

named her after *Dora the Explorer* because she had
been a stray who'd arrived on my doorstep. I told
them how they had loved *Dora the Explorer* when they
were small. It jogged a memory and Liam surprised
both of us when he began to sing the theme tune.
Dora, Dora, Dora, the Explorer. He could remember it.
It gave me hope that if we scratched a little deeper, he
would still have some memories of the time spent
with me locked in there somewhere.

We had several more FaceTime calls and then a
few weeks later I got a call from an unknown number.
I was shocked when I answered it to realise it was
Dan. *Uh-oh*, I thought. I guessed I was in trouble, although I couldn't think of anything I had said wrong.
I presumed I had overstepped the mark in some way
in my conversations with the boys but what he said
next totally caught me unawares. He explained that
he and Sylvie had been talking and that they wished
to invite me over for a week during the summer holidays. I had to ask him to repeat himself, sure that I
had misheard him, but again, he said that they
wanted to invite me to stay in their home for a week.
He explained that the boys had been asking a lot of
questions. They were curious about me and wanted
to get to know me a little better. He felt it would be
good for them to meet me again but this time without

the shock factor. He told me I could stay in one of the converted outbuildings where their guests usually stayed. I thanked him for the offer and told him I'd think about it. As soon as I had hung up I called in to Lucy next door and told her what had just happened. I longed to just say yes but I was scared. I was apprehensive about spending a week with them at their home under Dan and Sylvie's watch and I wouldn't even have Lucy around as my wingman but she persuaded me that if I wanted to get to know the boys and have a relationship with them, this was my chance and I needed to grab on to it with both hands.

'But what about Dora?' I argued. I hated the thought of leaving her alone for a week, but Lucy assured me that they would look after her and I knew I could trust her and Anabel to spoil Dora in my absence. Lucy told me that I couldn't afford to let my fear ruin this opportunity so I called Dan back the next day and agreed to come visit in July. Lucy helped me to book my flights and then there was no backing out. I was crossing off the days on the calendar that hung on my fridge, which one of the bin companies had put through the letter box at Christmastime. Usually, I had nothing to put on the calendar, no important dates or events to look forward to, but now I was putting an 'X' through each day, counting down the weeks until the day finally arrived for me to go to France. I kept Tim informed too; he knew about the journey to France and the exchange of letters afterwards. When I told him about Dan's invitation to stay with them, he punched the air with joy. I couldn't help but laugh. I think he was nearly happier for me than I was for myself.

As the weeks went by I was plagued by doubts but I was doing my best to flip the negatives into positives as I had learnt in my many years of counselling. As Lucy had reasoned, Dan and Sylvie wouldn't have invited me if they didn't feel it would benefit the boys. They must have been ready to take this step in our relationship. I just hoped my visit would be a positive experience for all of us.

When the day of my trip finally arrived, I woke up feeling awful. My stomach was knotted and my insides felt as though they had coagulated together during the night. I thought I might be coming down with something. 'It's just nerves,' Lucy had counselled when she saw me. 'You'll be fine, Eileen, I promise.'

I pulled my trolley across the tiles. The departures area was busy. Long queues snaked from desks, people rushed and hurried all around me, wheeling cases like mine and pushing trollies laden with luggage. Overtired children cried. Harried parents scolded. From my pocket I took out the sheet of paper that Lucy had given me with my instructions and unfolded it. She had written everything down for me. How and where I should check in, then I would go through security, then proceed to the gate to board the plane. The last time I had been on a plane was eighteen years ago when Dan and I had gone to Italy on our honeymoon. So much had changed since then. When I arrived in Marseille, Dan was going to meet me in the airport. Then the fun would really begin, I thought wryly.

As the plane ripped down the runway and we began to ascend up into the air, the houses and roads below becoming pieces in a miniature board game, I felt my chest tighten and my tummy constrict. My heart was racing. The air seemed to have left the cabin and I couldn't seem to pull it into my lungs. *What on earth was I doing?* I desperately wanted to shout, 'Stop!' I wanted to tell the pilot to get back on the ground again and let me off. That I had changed my mind about this.

I shoved my hands down into my pockets and there I found the comforter that Anabel had given me. I had put it in there to keep it safe. I wrapped my fingers around the fabric and gave it a squeeze. *Deep breaths*, I told myself. *You can do this.*

48

As I made my way to the arrivals hall, my heart ratcheted against my ribs like a small bird, fluttering inside a cage. My eyes roved over the crowd of people gathered there. I eventually spotted Dan standing just beyond the railings, but as I scanned the faces around him, I couldn't see the boys. I checked again but there was no sign of them. Acrid disappointment flooded through me as I wheeled my case behind me and made my way over to him.

'Where are the boys?' I asked, looking around.

'They're back at the house waiting for you but I thought it might be good for us to talk on our own first,' he explained.

I nodded, deep down knowing he was right but

feeling a sense of dread snake its way down my body. Wordlessly, I followed him towards the car park until we reached his Peugeot MPV. He unlocked the car and as I climbed into the passenger seat, I noticed that the back seat was littered with the boys' belongings: hoodies, water bottles and shin pads, all signs of a busy family life.

'Sorry about the mess,' Dan said, following my eyes. 'Life with boys.' He started the engine and proceeded towards the exit. 'So how was your flight?' he asked.

'Good. Good,' I replied as we both fell quiet again. The silence felt heavy between us, so thick you could cut through it with a pair of scissors, and I desperately scrambled for something to say to him. I hadn't expected to be alone with Dan without having the boys there as a distraction between us. I looked out the window at the flat-roofed warehouses and industrial units as we travelled along the motorway.

'I have to say I was surprised when you invited me to come,' I said eventually.

'The boys have been curious; they're asking a lot of questions about you... Sylvie and I thought this was the best way to handle it all.'

'Well, thank you, I really appreciate it.'

He paused and I knew there was something he wanted to say.

'Eileen?' he said eventually.

'Yes.'

'I think I owe you an apology.'

I glanced across the gearstick at him to make sure I had heard him properly.

'I don't think I gave you enough support back then. Sylvie reckons you probably had postnatal depression,' he continued.

I nodded. 'I think she's right.'

'It was only when she had Bastien that she realised the upheaval that came with being a new mother – the sleepless nights, the exhaustion...' he admitted. 'I don't know...' He sighed and shifted awkwardly in the driver's seat. 'Maybe I could have done more to help you... I tried to get you to go to the doctor, remember? But you wouldn't hear of it. You insisted you were coping just fine when really you weren't. Maybe I should have tried harder.'

I was taken aback by the admission. 'Look, Dan, it was a long time ago.' I would never forgive him for allowing me to be erased out of my sons' lives but I had to accept a lot of the responsibility for what had happened. 'I guess we've both made mistakes,' I conceded.

We both fell silent for the rest of the journey, each lost in our own thoughts. I looked out the window at the passing scenery. As we drove deeper into the Provence countryside, the industrial estates gave way to rolling fields. Everything looked different now to when I had visited at Easter; mauve carpets of lavender fields sloped gently on both sides of the road. The vines were sagging with ripe fruit and the earth was scorched and dusty.

Eventually, we arrived at the farmhouse and entered through the pillars. The tyres crunched over the gravel and as soon as Dan had silenced the engine, the boys hurried out to greet us. They had grown taller since I had last seen them; they were almost as tall as Dan now and they were more tanned too. The sun was blistering hot as I stepped out of the car. Although I dearly longed to pull them into a hug, I wasn't sure if it was appropriate so instead I made do with a greeting in the French way, a kiss on both cheeks. Sylvie followed after them and greeted me in the same manner. She told me I was welcome and spoke to the boys in English and told them to show me to the cottage where I would be staying.

Liam took my small case from the boot and I followed him across the courtyard. My room was simple and rustic. Exposed timber beams supported the low ceilings and thick stone walls kept the inside cool. A double bed clothed in starched white bed linen standing in the centre of the room and a small bedside table were the only furniture. I moved over to the window and saw it had beautiful views down the hillside. A sprig of lavender lay on my pillow top. Although I didn't know if it was Sylvie who had left it there, it felt like the kind of thing a woman would do. Whoever had done it, it was a nice touch and I was grateful.

The boys left me to freshen up and told me to meet for dinner on the terrace when I was ready. I fired off a quick message to Lucy to see how Dora was. I was getting to grips with my new phone; it was very easy once you figured it out. She replied instantly, almost as if she'd been waiting with her phone in her hand. I watched the three dots bouncing on the screen as she typed a reply. Finally, her message arrived to say that Dora was living her best life and Anabel was already giving her so many bad habits. I laughed as I read it. It sounded as though Dora was having a great time. She asked me how it was all going and I told her so far, so good and that I had been made to feel welcome.

I splashed my face with water, then changed into a red sundress with a daisy print, that Lucy had helped me to purchase the week before. We had looked up the weather forecast for Provence and saw it was set to hit thirty degrees so we had gone into town and bought shorts, T-shirts and a few light dresses. I checked my appearance in the mirror; I had to admit that Lucy was right, the colour did suit me. Almost all my clothes were either black or grey and she had talked me into wearing some brighter colours for a change. I looked younger somehow; the colour lifted my face and gave me a badly needed confidence boost.

I emerged from my cottage, made my way across the courtyard to the terrace beside the house as Liam had told me to do. Although it was early evening, the sun still sat heavy in the sky. There were no birds in the air or even a whisper of a breeze to be felt. Not even an insect moved beneath the oppressive sun. Two long wooden benches ran along either side of the table which had been set with starched white linen and pale blue crockery. After a moment, the three boys emerged from the house with bowls of salad and put them in the centre of the table. I noticed they had changed from the T-shirts they had been wearing earlier and were now wearing shirts. Sylvie followed after them with a serving dish containing cod served with a tomato and olive sauce and we all sat down. Dan brought out the wine. There was a basket of fresh bread flavoured with rosemary and seasoned with salt. My stomach betrayed me and began to growl audibly at the sight of all the delicious food. I realised I was starving. I had been too anxious and as a result I had eaten nothing all day. I tucked into the delectable spread, savouring the flavours, the juicy sun-ripened tomatoes, the fragrant herbs Sylvie had used in the sauce. It had been a long time since I had eaten food so good. Sylvie poured me a glass of chilled white wine and I nearly fell off my chair when she handed the boys a mini glass too. I tried not to appear shocked; I knew the French had their own way of doing things. We chatted generally to one another. They spoke English and I was grateful that they were making an effort for my sake. Sylvie asked about my life in Dublin and what the weather was like in Ireland at the moment. I felt myself relax as we chatted easily with one another. Dan told me they had guests staying in some of the other cottages. Sometimes they would join them for dinner but that evening they had all gone into Lourmarin for dinner so we had the terrace to ourselves.

I looked around the landscape as we sat under the dying sun. The vines were weighed down with fruit as far as the eye could see and the gnarled roots of olive trees searched out water deep within the scorched earth. I couldn't tell what Dan and Sylvie were thinking but the boys seemed to be enjoying having me there. As the others talked, Eoghan and I fell into conversation together and he asked me what he had been like as a baby. I told him that he had been the cutest baby and that his hair had been a much brighter red. He seemed surprised and told me he had never seen a photo of himself as a baby. I was shocked. I wondered what had happened to all the photos I had taken of them and put into albums. I guessed they had got lost in the move from Ireland or perhaps Dan had hidden them away somewhere, fearing they might come across a photo with me in it and start asking questions.

We stayed up late into the night. Sylvie kept my wine topped up as we talked and laughed. Dan and I even reminisced about the boys as babies and they adored hearing the stories of the mischief they had got up to and the funny things they had said. Even Sylvie laughed when I told them about the time Liam had drawn all over Eoghan's face with green permanent marker and how it had taken weeks for it to fade. As we talked about the past, there was no lingering tension or bitterness like I had feared. I realised that it wasn't just the boys who seemed happy, *I* was happy here too. And relaxed.

The boys teased Bastien mercilessly and the banter between them was a good distraction for the grown-ups. They wrestled with him, pulled out his chair as he went to sit down, and ate his food if he turned his back on his plate for even a moment, but it was good-natured. They clearly adored their younger brother and there was so much warmth and love between them all. I was glad that the revelation that Bastien was only their half-brother didn't seem to have affected their relationship.

Somewhere during the evening I realised that the bonds that came with birthing them had dissolved a long time ago and they would never see me as a mother. It dawned on me with a bittersweet tinge of regret, that *this* was their family now – this was where they belonged. I could never try to uproot them – I wouldn't *want* to uproot them from this. This was where they were happy. Through Dan and Sylvie's kindness I could be a part of their extended family if I wanted. They had welcomed me here and I could either take the hand they had reached out to me or I could spend my whole life fighting for more and risk alienating them altogether; it was up to me. If this worked out, perhaps I could visit more regularly and, who knew, in the future, maybe when the boys were a little older and Dan trusted me more, they might even be allowed to come visit me in Ireland.

I realised that I would never have a conventional relationship with my sons; there was too much water under the bridge for that, but after so many years apart, I could be happy with this – this was far more than I could have ever imagined as I had lain on my bed back in St Jude's dreaming of the day we might meet again. Being a part of their family was enough for me. Life was messy and complicated, families even more so. I thought about Lucy and how she had thought she and Neil would be together forever, but life had a funny way of turning the tables and surprising you when you least expected it. You could either pick yourself up, reset and try again or you could let it define the rest of your life. For so long I had done that. I had been beholden to fear; I had spent too many years allowing my guilt for what I had done to punish me, but slowly, through Lucy's help, I was learning to forgive myself. The old me was starting to return again. Slowly, step by step, I was healing. This blended family was mine and I realised it was perfect in its own way. I was very grateful for another chance and I was going to hold on to it with both hands.

ACKNOWLEDGMENTS

What a joy it is to get to this stage! No matter how many books I write, it is a privilege to be able to thank the people that help bring the book from my head, out into the world.

Firstly, to my agent Hannah Todd from the Madeleine Milburn Agency, the best of the best. Thank you as always for your enthusiasm, positivity, and guidance with this book.

A huge thank you is also due to my editor, Caroline Ridding, who is always so encouraging and kind in her feedback. Now, after four books together, Caroline, I can hear your voice as I write. I'm so excited to continue working with you. To Candida Bradford for her superb copy-edit which has benefitted this book so greatly, and also to Ross Dickinson for his proof-reading skills, it was a pleasure to work with you again, Ross.

Thanks are also due to the wonderful team at Boldwood. You continue to get bigger and better, yet treat your authors with so much individual care and attention. You all work so hard, I feel so grateful to be part of the team.

My fellow Boldwood authors are always so supportive too, and I am extremely grateful to Clare Swatman for taking the time to correct my appalling French in this book. Merci, Clare!

To all the booksellers, bloggers and libraries for their support.

I am so thankful every day that I get to do this for a living, so thank you to my readers, especially those people who leave reviews and contact me with lovely messages and kind words, you'll never know how much those messages mean.

To my family and friends for always cheering me on and lastly to my gang: my husband Simon and our four beautiful children, Lila, Tom, Bea and Charlie – how lucky am I! You make me prouder with every day and I am so grateful for you all.

MORE FROM CAROLINE FINNERTY

We hope you enjoyed reading *The Family Next Door*. If you did, please leave a review.

If you'd like to gift a copy, this book is also available as an ebook, paperback, hardback, digital audio download and audiobook CD.

Sign up to Caroline Finnerty's mailing list for news, competitions and updates on future books.

http://bit.ly/CarolineFinnertyNewsletter

Explore more heart-wrenching family dramas from Caroline Finnerty...

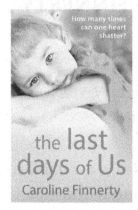

How many times can one heart shatter?

the last days of Us

Caroline Finnerty

Little secrets grow up into BIG lies...

a mother's secret

Caroline Finnerty

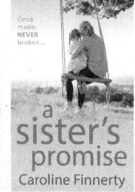

Once made, NEVER broken...

a sister's promise

Caroline Finnerty

ABOUT THE AUTHOR

Caroline Finnerty is an Irish author of heart-wrenching family dramas and has published four novels and compiled a non-fiction charity anthology. She has been shortlisted for several short-story awards and lives in County Kildare with her husband and four young children.

Visit Caroline's Website: www.carolinefinnerty.ie

twitter.com/cfinnertywriter

facebook.com/carolinefinnertywriter

instagram.com/carolinefinnerty

goodreads.com/carolinefinnerty

bookbub.com/profile/caroline-finnerty

Boldwood

Boldwood Books is an award-winning fiction publishing company seeking out the best stories from around the world.

Find out more at www.boldwoodbooks.com

Join our reader community for brilliant books, competitions and offers!

Follow us
@BoldwoodBooks
@BookandTonic

Sign up to our weekly deals newsletter

https://bit.ly/BoldwoodBNewsletter

Milton Keynes UK
Ingram Content Group UK Ltd.
UKHW041826070823
426482UK00003B/107